RIDE WITH A REBEL

RIDE WITH A REBEL

Jack Holman

To order additional copies of this book, contact:
Xlibris Corporation
1-888-795-4274
www.Xlibris.com
Orders@Xlibris.com
37683

CONTENTS

DEDICATION

During the early 1950's, my bride, Mildred (Miekie), devoted hours on end to typing on a mechanical typewriter, Jesse Roderick Sparkman's Civil War Diary. Our weekly newspaper, THE MACON BEACON, wrote the diary in segments. It is a good thing that Miekie copied the diary because the old "Home Place" burned and the diary went up in smoke. Miekie prepared "ditto" copies and gave them to family.

In the 1980's, Miekie and I, with her mother, Sallie Doris Killebrew, drove a motor home to almost all of the battlefields on which Jesse fought. We made photographs, talked with park rangers, historians, and walked throughout the grounds.

I began to write Jesse's story as it came through to me. Sallie Doris was Jesse's granddaughter. Miekie pressed me to publish RIDE WITH A REBEL.

Thus, I dedicate this book with love and hugs to Miekie and Sallie Doris.

Introduction
To
Ride With A Rebel

"The Official Confederate Military Records" on file in Mississippi's Department of Archives and History confirm that Jesse Roderick Sparkman was a member of the Jeff Davis Legion of Mississippi Cavalry, CSA (Confederate States of America). He served in Company C.

Jesse wrote a consistent account of his life while with the cavalry. Unfortunately the original diary was destroyed when a family home burned. Before the loss occurred *The Macon Beacon* printed the entire document. Mildred Killebrew Holman, Jesse's great granddaughter, typed a copy. Some of the words were not decipherable due to abuse to which it had been subjected during the war.

My imagination ran wild while I read Jesse's diary. His words told haunting events to me. I placed maps on my desk and plotted his travels, most of which he covered while riding a horse.

During 1985, Mildred, Doris Holladay Killebrew (Jesse's granddaughter), and I drove to most battle sites of Jesse's experiences. I photographed the battlefields, bought historical documents which described battles, and I wrote to The Library of Congress. I studied their original photographs and artists' paintings, Battles and Leaders of the Civil War, Harper's Weekly, and National Archives. I interviewed historians and prepared tapes of their comments.

My father served as a cavalry officer during World War I. When I was knee-high to a horse, he taught me to ride, care for, and love the scent of horse flesh.

I served almost three years in the U.S. Navy during World War II. I watched a German submarine burst open and sink after the USS Hobson's guns fired. The Hobson was flagship for a destroyer division while the Allies invaded Normandy on D-Day, 6, June, 1944. The Hobson gave fire support at the Southern France Invasion on 15, August, 1944.

And then, our U.S. Navy converted the USS Hobson into a high speed, destroyer mine sweeper. She steamed through the Panama Canal and into the Pacific Ocean. After practice, practice, practice, and drills, drills, drills, the Hobson helped clear the Okinawa Invasion channel. Japanese soldiers and Kamikaze Planes defended the island furiously. After the invasion, the Hobson steamed on a radar picket station until 16, April, 1945, when Kamikazes attacked her and the USS Pringle, a destroyer. The Pringle took a hit, caved-in and sank. A bomb and a Kamikaze's engine hit the Hobson.

I know the emotions and horrors of war. With those in mind, I wrote the story Jesse told me. Actions packed many life-threatening minutes for him. He spent some "bone-dry," time.

If you enjoy reading United States' history, with a lively touch, I think you will enjoy RIDE WITH A REBEL.

JOIN THE CONFEDERATE ARMY

JUNE, 1861

SATURDAY/15th. Jesse Roderick Sparkman, now nineteen years old, spurred his horse's side. Sam, a slender, iron-gray thoroughbred, galloped from a green cotton field. His hooves beat upon a path which followed the Noxubee River. In the shade of a huge cypress a fish line bent a willow limb. The freckle-faced Jesse jumped from Sam and ran to the river's edge. He lifted the willow limb. An old turtle's eyes opened slowly. "Sam, perhaps this isn't the best fishing hole on the river, but it's a great place for me to sit down and do some serious thinking. Okay?"

Slave's voices chanted melodious notes in rhythm with the chop, chop, chop of their hoes. Inquiring perch splashed from rippling waters. A moccasin slithered from its resting place atop a sunny log and swam away. A shiny crow cawed and flew from the cypress.

Jesse's icy-blue eyes scanned the far side of the river while he took a crinkled piece of paper from his shirt pocket. He unfolded the paper and studied its contents. His lips moved. "JOIN THE CONFEDERATE ARMY."

He visualized riding Sam, confronting and shooting a Yankee horseman. His heart beat a little faster. Sweat trickled down his cheeks when he thought about a Yankee's sword piercing his own stomach and blood oozing out. "Sam, if I join the army, I may never see this plantation again. I reckon Pa can manage it without me."

A small man who wore black trousers, supported with red suspenders over a white shirt, ambled along the river's bank. He whistled tuneless notes, carried a cane pole in one hand and a basket in the other. "Oh. Hello, Jesse, you startled me. I suppose the current is too swift for fish to bite."

"You're probably right, Dr. Spencer. William Daniel told me what you said about our slaves." Jesse straightened the reins along Sam's neck.

"Plantation owners insist that you must have slaves with which to farm, and our constitution guarantees individual freedom. Slaves are individuals." Dr. Spencer frowned.

Jesse's face crimsoned. "I've studied about your Pennsylvania's industrialists, and their enslaving laborers. Those people live in atrocious company settlements, governed by bosses. Our slaves have more freedom than your northern laborers and you know it."

"Jesse, it was absolutely senseless for South Carolina, and Mississippi, and all the others to secede from the Union. This country must function under one constitution or fail miserably."

"What about states' rights to govern themselves?" Jesse placed his boot into a stirrup.

"States must govern themselves in a manner which does not conflict with the Federal Constitution." Dr. Spencer looked over his little eye glasses which sat upon the middle of his nose.

"What does the Constitution say about interstate commerce? There is no national justice in our railroads and waterways charging higher rates for us to ship goods north than those same goods moving south."

Dr. Spencer sat at the river's edge and baited a hook. "If those same southern delegates who met in Montgomery and formed a new government had gone to Washington they could have worked out the rates."

Jesse swung into his saddle and tightened the reins with large, sun-tanned hands. "President Davis told the whole world that all we want is to be left alone."

Dr. Spencer spit on a hook and swung the bait into a rippling river. "Yes, but all hope for a peaceful secession vanished in the cannon smoke after South Carolina Confederates opened fire on Fort Sumpter."

"When I was a little boy, my family moved from Beaufort County, North Carolina. I keep picturing, in my mind's eye, many cannons along the shoreline. I constantly hear a soldier shout, 'READY. FIRE.' Fire spits from each cannon, loud blasts shatter the silence, clouds of smoke drift with the wind, and cannon balls splash into the blue water."

Dr. Spencer adjusted his glasses. "Yes, and did you know that the bombardment continued thirty-four hours without a single man's shedding any blood?"

"The Confederacy told the United States that all its military installations must be removed from the South, but President Lincoln refused their order. Instead, he issued a call for 75,000 men. We took that to mean a formal declaration of war. I don't believe the Rebels intended to kill."

Jesse's lips parted. Pearl-white teeth reflected the sun. His eyes squinted and tiny wrinkles formed at their corners. He sat upright in his saddle and squared his shoulders. "Sam and I are going to fight a war to set us free from the Federals."

"You are making a big mistake, Jesse."

Jesse returned to the cotton fields. Sweat dripped from the slaves' faces and drenched their clothing. Jesse sensed the foul odor from their bodies and rode up-wind to survey their progress. He adjusted his hat until shade covered his eyes.

That evening, Jesse joined his mother and father for supper. Samantha, a sixteen year old slave-girl, dressed in a starched, white uniform, stacked plates for Mr. Sparkman. She said, "Mr. Jesse, you didn't eat but one biscuit."

Jesse looked from face to face. "I plan to join the cavalry."

"Now. Now, Jesse. You are too young. You've got your whole life before you." His mother touched his hand.

Mr. Sparkman packed tobacco into his pipe. He looked at the match. Slowly, he drawled, "A man's got to do what he believes in, or else he ain't much of a man."

"Several of my friends have already joined and I believe I should do my part." Jesse walked from the table to their large front porch. He tossed a blue pillow against one end of the swing and lay down. The swing creaked, sparrows began to roost in the vines, and a turtle-dove crooned its love song.

MONDAY/17th. Facing his father and mother who sat quietly at the table, Jesse smiled. "Good morning, Ma . . . Pa. This is gonna be a good day for riding."

Samantha grinned, carrying a plate filled with fried eggs. "Well. Mista Jesse, you better enjoy this food, 'cause from now on, you might have to fix it yourself."

"Aw, Samantha, we'll have good cooks for the cavalry, but I'm sure they can't cook like this."

Samantha stopped by his side and placed her hands on her hips. "We sho will miss you, but lawd have mercy, we sho won't have to do near the cookin' we have to do when you is here."

"I'm still a growing boy, Samantha." He raked two more fried eggs onto his plate and handed the empty platter to her.

The grandfathers clock gonged six times. Jesse's eyes met his mother and father's. "Please excuse me."

Jesse shoved his chair from the table, lifted saddlebags to his shoulder, and said, "I'd best be on the road if I'll be in Scooba by noon. Pa, you said that you might want to ride with me. Are you going?"

"Yes . . . I am. I want to see you off and I can take care of some business while in town. The boys have saddled our horses."

While walking to the stable, Jesse placed an arm around his mother's waist. He paused and looked at a field of cotton. "If the weather holds up, we ought to have a bumper crop this year. Maybe the war will be over and I'll be home to help with the ginning."

His mother placed her hand over his. "I don't see much chance for it to be over by fall, but I do hope you can be home."

Jesse wrapped his arms around her and his muscles bulged as he held her close. He kissed her cheek and smiled.

His father and Jesse mounted their horses and rode along the oak shrouded lane, toward the main road. The older Sparkman broke their silence. "I remember letting you ride horseback when you were no more than three years old. You kicked ol' Nellie in her sides and shook the bridle. She just walked the path beside our home in Carolina. You got furious when she went to her feed box instead going out on the road."

Jesse said, "I've loved horses for as long as I can remember and I've raised Sam from a colt."

A hand-made sign, nailed to a large oak tree, read, "Lemonade—Penny A Glass."

Sallie Denton ran to the edge of the road. Her tiny fingers twisted a pink ribbon tied to a "pig-tail" in her hair. Her dark brown eyes twinkled as she smiled. "You can be my first customers."

"How was everything in Geiger when you left it?" Jesse reined Sam to a stop.

Sallie nestled a rag doll to her shoulder. "Geiger's fine and I'm so glad to be out of school. How many glasses do you want to buy?"

"I'm pretty thirsty and Pa needs a glass. Let me have two to start." Jesse handed a nickel to her.

"I don't have any change. I reckon you'll have to drink fives glasses between you. Jesse, let me ride Sam."

Jesse said, "Today, time is running a little short. Sam and I joined the Confederate Cavalry and we've got to be in Scooba by noon."

She looked puzzled. "What's the cavalry, Jesse?"

"The cavalry is a large bunch of horsemen who play hide and seek with the Yankee's Army. I've changed my mind. You can ride with me down yonder and back to that lone pine tree."

"Oh. Thank you." She grasped Jesse's wrist.

Gently, he lifted her and placed her behind his saddle. Her small arms squeezed him while they galloped toward the pine. She spoke into Jesse's ear. "You aren't going to war, are you?"

"I reckon I am but it won't be for very long." He spurred Sam.

"Will you write to me?" Sallie placed a hand on his shoulder.

"I'll write every time you write to me. And we can make believe you are my sweetheart. How old are you?"

"I'm eleven." She tucked the rag doll into Jesse's shirt pocket. "Keep Madge close to your heart and she'll protect you."

At the front gate she jumped from Sam's back. Her eyes met Jesse's. Suddenly, she hugged his leg. "Don't forget to write. I don't want you to go to war. I don't know what it's all about but I'm scared."

Tears trickled down her cheeks. She ran toward the house. Jesse spurred Sam and caught up with the older Sparkman.

Jesse saw other men mounted on their horses, milling about the Scooba school grounds. He said, "Looks like a few mothers and lady friends are here to see us off. But fathers make-up most of the crowd."

A man dressed in a Confederate uniform circled his hand above his head. "I'm Captain Perrin. May I have your attention, please?"

"Son, I'm mighty proud that you're willing to fight for what you believe in. Good-bye, now." The older Sparkman shook Jesse's hand.

"Good-bye, Pa. I love y'all." He turned Sam and rode beside Captain Perrin.

"Men, I am your commanding officer. Welcome to the Jeff Davis Legion. We'll form up and ride in columns of two. Find a partner and y'all stay together from here on. It's half past twelve and Union City, Tennessee, is a long ways from Scooba, Mississippi. Follow me."

The men kissed their wives and sweethearts. Some exchanged hand-shakes with friends and relatives. Women dabbed handkerchiefs to their eyes.

Jesse rode to William Daniel and said, "I think we'll make a good pair. Is that all right?"

"You've got to be tough to stay up with me." William grinned.

"Company C. Forward. MARCH." Captain Perrin galloped his sorrel thoroughbred onto the dusty road leading north. The riders fell in behind him. Saddle bags bounced behind each saddle.

After galloping for approximately one mile, Perrin began a slower pace. He used the two gaits until almost dark. At the outskirts of a town he stopped his horse in a church yard. "Men. We're approaching West Point, Mississippi.

We'll eat supper in a little tavern, feed our horses, and continue to ride. I'll pay for your meals."

TUESDAY/18. Company C rode into Corinth, just as the sun peeked over the horizon.

At camp near Union City, these men swarmed throughout the grounds where thousands of men and horses assembled. Captain Perrin shouted,

"FALL IN. This will be our home for training. We'll get some tents from the quartermaster. You men that rode together sleep together."

Jesse and William stretched out their tent and drove stakes into the ground. Sweat dripped from their noses. William said, "I don't know about you, but I'm saddle sore."

"Looks like some of these boys came from the city and don't know how to set up tents. Let's give a helping hand." Jesse walked toward a tent which covered two wiggling humps and gurgling voices.

"Hurry up and finish with them tents." A sergeant shouted. "We gotta be in that chow line over yonder in fifteen minutes. You're just messing around. Let's go. Let's go."

"I'm about to get a belly full of that guy and we just got here." William spoke in low tones.

"Yeah. He could become a burr under a saddle. We're gonna have to learn to live with him." Jesse placed a blade of grass into his mouth. He lifted his saddlebag from the tent and removed a shiny metal plate and cup.

"Don't forget your knife, fork, and spoon." William tossed his bag into the tent.

"Look at the length of that line. All I need is a harmonica to play while you shake your tin cup, and we could make a little spendin' money." Jesse cleaned his fork with a handkerchief.

Sergeant yelled, "Find a place under a shade tree. When you're finished eating, wash your gear in them cans settin' over yonder. The first one's soapy water; the other scaldin'. We don't want nobody catchin' dysentery."

"This hard tack ain't bad with beans poured over it." Jesse scraped his plate.

"I'll race you back to our tent." William dipped his gear into the scalding water.

"These tents look like sway-back horses." Jesse adjusted a tent pole while William tightened a guy-line.

A bugle sounded and soldiers scurried to the flagpole. Sergeant ordered, "All right men, we gotta move ammunition from them wagons over yonder, into the warehouse. The wind is blowing soft from the south and that means rain. Don't let me see nobody draggin'. Double quick time."

WEDNESDAY/19. Notes from a bugle blared. Sergeant yelled, "Reveille. Reveille. Git up and git moving. You've got twenty minutes to be at breakfast. Move it. Move it."

After breakfast Sergeant ordered, "Y'all follow me and I'll take you to the doctor. They'll check you over. You gotta be in top shape to stay in this outfit."

After his examination a medic told Jesse, "You're near about perfect. The quartermaster is down yonder. He'll equip you with two uniforms and all the other stuff. If you get sick or injured sick call is every morning at 8:00."

"I won't get sick." Jesse smiled.

The quartermaster looked at Jesse and said, "I ain't got no uniform to fit a man your size. You'll have to make-do until we get in a new shipment. Where did you come from?"

"Mississippi." He leaned over and stuffed a pair of boots into his new saddlebag. Madge, the rag doll, fell to the ground silently.

"Lookie here." The quartermaster waited. "This Mississippi boy has got to have his rag doll so he can be bye-bye from home."

Jesse blushed. His fist thudded against the quartermaster's jaw. All 240 pounds lay motionless on the floor. The crowd hushed. Jesse placed Madge into his shirt pocket and walked to his tent.

"Get your rifle." Sergeant opened the flap. "It's a good thing you ain't got no rank, or else you'd be busted for hittin' a non-commissioned officer. Maybe a long walk on the drill field will learn you to cool your temper."

"Word travels fast. I didn't see you at the quartermaster's." Jesse lifted his rifle.

"How come you hit the man about a little ol' doll? Are you a lily?"

"I've got my reasons," Jesse wiped sweat from his brow.

"Hold that rifle straight up, over your head. Don't bend them elbows. Run around the outside edges of this here field until I tell you to stop. Any questions?"

"No, Sir."

Sergeant lit and puffed a cigar. He blew a blast of smoke into Jesse's eyes.

"You didn't have to do that."

"Don't tell me what I ain't suppose to do. Run, soldier, RUN."

Summer's sun bore down. Sweat drenched Jesse's shirt. He lowered the rifle and removed his shirt.

"That'll cost you five more laps around the field. Who told you to undress?"

"Nobody."

"Until you get to be Somebody, don't you listen to Nobody. I tell you what you can and cannot do. Do you understand?"

"Yes, Sir."

"Run, Soldier, Run. Lift that rifle higher."

Jesse gulped a cup of water when he and William walked into headquarters. "He better not ever be in a battle with me. I'll kill him."

"You said that we've got to put up with him. While you were marching with that silly rifle over your head, I found out that Sergeant will be responsible for drilling our company two hours each morning on horseback, and two hours each evening on foot. It's his job to push every man to his breaking point, and every man has one." William sipped his water.

"One good thing about this camp is our food and feed for our horses." He gulped another cup of water.

SUNDAY/23. At daybreak, Company C rode and formed up at the headquarters' flagpole. Captain Perrin and Sergeant marched back and forth, stopping occasionally in front of a soldier. Sergeant's beady, black eyes squinted as they began at Jesse's cap and searched down his face, over his chest, trousers, and shoes.

"Private Sparkman. Your rifle is dirty. Jus' plain dirty . . . dirty. Fall out and run ten laps around the drill field. Clean up that rifle and be ready to march to the depot by eight. Is that clear?"

"Yes, Sir."

At 8:00 Jesse and William mounted their horses and galloped with the company to Union City railroad station. Captain Perrin rode the front; Sergeant the side. Sam, Jesse's horse, was third from the front in column one. William rode next to them, in column two. Their bedrolls bounced behind their saddles. Lather formed on the horses' necks.

"HALT." Captain Perrin wiped sweat from his forehead. "Men. This is a drill. The depot is full to capacity with ammunition and our assignment is to protect it from the south. Privates Daniel and Sparkman will ride picket for four hours and be replaced by Pettus and Caskell."

Jesse and William rode south along the railroad tracks for nearly a mile. William nodded his head to his right. "Don't look now but I see some soldiers marching rout-step through those woods."

"Capt'n Perrin said our enemy would be wearing red armbands and that's what I see. I'm sure they see us. We're in the wide open. Let's ride parallel to their front until we get to those houses; then work our way back to the company."

The blue battalion formed into a huge U-shape, camouflaged into trees and shrubs. The red battalion marched into the trap. Blackpowder smoke belched from a circle of muskets. The reds were identified as killed, wounded, and surrendered by field judges.

MONDAY/24. Captain Perrin assembled the company at sunset. "Men. I don't believe in long speeches. We beat our enemy here, but this wasn't real war. We're going back to camp tonight, and I want you to be ready for drill in the morning. Sergeant, head em' out."

JULY, 1861

TUESDAY/23. Company C prepared to leave camp. They rode their horses to the depot.

WEDNESDAY/24. At nightfall, Captain Perrin assembled the company. "Men, we will ride to Iuka, Mississippi, and camp about a half mile out. Mount-up."

THURSDAY/25. Company C reached Iuka at 2:00 in the morning. Five of the boys became sick. Captain Perrin said, "Jesse, I'm pretty sure they have camp fever. We don't want this fever to spread; so you ride with them to the tavern and attend to them. Find a doctor."

"Private Sparkman, this fever is very contagious." The doctor stood at his office window and looked out. "We'll keep three boys in one room and two in another, at the tavern. You can stay in a room by yourself and take part in company drills. Hopefully, you won't catch it."

AUGUST, 1861

THURSDAY/1. Captain Perrin handed furloughs to each man of Company C. "All of you men from Noxubee County will board railroad cars and reach Macon tomorrow night. Leave whiskey and women alone and don't mess up."

Jesse stuffed his bag. He smiled at Madge and straightened her mussed-up hair. With furlough in hand he boarded a rail car.

FRIDAY/2. Jesse stepped from the train in Macon, Mississippi. He walked inside the depot at 9:00 P.M. and saw several drivers of rigs. "Hey, Woodrow. Can I hire you to drive me to Cooksville??

"Yes, Sir, Mr. Jesse. Where're your bags?"

SATURDAY/3. In the wee morning hours, Jesse jumped from the rig and paid Woodrow. "The air even smells good in Noxubee County. I can't tell much about the way our crops look."

"They're fine, Mr. Jesse. Last week, I brought some cotton baskets for your daddy. Y'all's cotton is something to be proud of."

"You've got a long drive back into town. I won't hold you up. Good night."

The rig's wheels glistened in the moonlight. Jesse's boot hit a step and he stumbled across the front porch. Boards creaked. The screen door slammed behind him. He yelled, "Is anybody home?"

"Is that you, Jesse?"

"Yes, Sir."

"We weren't looking for you until tomorrow." Pa Sparkman lit a lamp. "Come on back."

"I wanted to surprise y'all. Our furloughs are good for one week; then I report back to the company. I'm excited about the cavalry and will tell you all about my experiences."

Ma Sparkman hugged him. "Good night, Jesse. We'll see you in the morning."

SEPTEMBER, 1861

WEDNESDAY/4. Company C remained in Iuka until early morning. Jesse reached home late at night.

Ma Sparkman placed her arms around his neck and kissed him. She stepped back. "You're burning up with fever. What's the matter with you?"

"I'm fine, Ma, and I'm so glad to be home." He plopped into a large rocking chair. "I've had a long train ride and it's late now. I'll let y'all get back to bed, and I'll tell all about the cavalry when I wake up. I want to sleep, sleep, sleep."

"Your bed is made up. Samantha put clean sheets and pillow cases on it today." Ma yawned.

A great big smile crept across his face, he reached behind his neck and untied a pale blue kerchief. "I feel the touch of fall. The morning air is a little cooler, and daylight is shorter."

Carefully, Ma tip-toed into Jesse's room. He lay soundly asleep. She stood at the foot of his bed. She touched a tear in her eye. "Our little boy is a grown man now. Lord, how can you let him go off to a cruel war like this? I beg your protection over him."

"What'd you say, Ma?"

"Nothing. Nothing at all. I must have been thinking out loud."

THURSDAY/5. In the dawn's early light Ma sat on the edge of his bed. She held his sunburned hand, placed her thumb against his, her fingers to his. "Your hand looks like a lion's paw against a kitty cat's. Beads of sweat are all over your face. You've still got a high fever."

"Just wait till after breakfast. I'm fine."

"Well. All right. Pa's gone to look over some cotton fields. Our crop is the best we've had for several years. Stalks are higher than your stirrups and loaded with open bolls.

Samantha brought fresh honey and hot biscuits with butter to the table. Jesse ate four fried eggs, four pieces of bacon, three huge biscuits, and two glasses of milk. He pushed back from the table. "This beats the cavalry's food, Samantha."

"Pa said for you to ride Nellie. Y'all are to meet at the water trough at eight o'clock. Ma helped stack the dishes.

After a short ride, Jesse saw Pa in a field of unpicked cotton. Pa said, "I didn't hear you. I was fixin' to meet you at the water trough. Let's ride to the field over yonder. We've got fifty pickers in it.

"Are cotton prices good?"

"The mills in South Carolina are paying top prices and running at peak production. They want you boys to have the best uniforms for winter. You look pale."

"I reckon I've got camp fever. Dry heaves go along with it. I'm gonna ride back to the house. Y'all let Samantha take care of me and I'll tell her what to do."

That afternoon, Samantha rocked in a large chair near an open window. Starched white curtains moved gently.

"Samantha. Please bring a bucket of cold spring water to me. This fever is burning me up, but I feel like I'm freezing."

Samantha set the bucket on a bedside table. "Anything else, Mr. Jesse?"

"No thanks. Stay as far away from me as you can, and after you touch anything I use wash your hands with lye soap." He soaked a small towel in the water and wrapped it around his head. While in a deep sleep, he tossed and tumbled. His eyes opened but didn't focus. They were shiny.

"I'm on fire. Water. Water." He saturated the towel.

"Mr. Jesse. Wake up. It's after five. I've got some soup for you. You been sleep all day." Samantha placed a tray on the bedside table.

"Thanks." He ate a little of the soup. "Get out, Samantha. I'm sick to my stomach."

That night, Samantha set up a cot in the hall and lay down.

"Samantha. Please bring me some spring water. I'm burning up." He raised his head from the pillow while she lit a lamp.

"Yes, Sir," She tip-toed from the house.

FRIDAY/6. Ma walked into his room at dawn. She straightened his sheets and put on dry pillow slips. "How do you feel?"

"You'd better not come near me or else you'll catch this fever."

"I've done enough nursing in my day to know how to keep from catching your fever. I'm going to the kitchen and fix some milk toast for you."

"My fever's down." Jesse stood. "The room is going around and aroun'. Where're my trousers?"

Ma and Samantha helped him stagger back into bed. He fell asleep immediately.

SATURDAY/7 The doctor said, "You've been a mighty sick soldier, Jesse." The doctor counted pulse. "You've got to stay in bed a little longer. I'll leave some medicine with Ma."

"Thanks, Doc. I'm fine. Go and 'tend to other sick folks. I've got to report for duty."

SUNDAY/15. After dinner Jesse relaxed on the front porch swing. While he slept Samantha held Sallie Denton's horse. Sallie smiled and said, "Thank you."

She tip-toed toward the porch steps and saw a white feather on the grass. Using the feather, she tickled Jesse's lips. He made a funny face. She tickled his lips again and he slapped the feather. She laughed loudly.

"What are you laughing at and where did you come from? Am I dreaming?" Jesse squinted a half open eye.

"I'm laughing at the funny faces you make when you sleep." She sat on his stomach.

"When did you get to Cooksville?"

"Mother and I came yesterday. Thomas Permenter was sick and died this morning. He had a congestive chill. Whatever that is. They are burying him Tuesday.

"Thomas died? I left him at a tavern in Iuka, and he was feeling better."

"The grown folks kind of turned away from me when they talked about him." Sallie looked at Jesse. "Have you ever seen a dead person?"

"I've seen two or three."

"What are they like?"

"The ones I've seen look as if they're asleep. Let me tell you the way I see death. First off, nobody fully understands it. We who are Christians are taught that death is simply the end of our life on Earth. Our souls which we can't see go to Heaven and live with God. Heaven is greater than anything we can imagine. Our family and friends will all be there. Golden streets shine, homes protect us. Our dogs will lick our faces and hands. Horses move faster than the wind. Whatever causes you happiness here will be there. Thomas doesn't have to worry about getting shot and hurt or killed. He's gone on to Heaven and will be waiting for us."

"His funeral will be at the Cooksville Church cemetery. Do you feel well enough to go?"

"I'm leaving in the morning." He looked into her questioning eyes. "We muster in Tuesday, and arrive in Richmond, Virginia on the 19th. I'll visit Thomas' family this afternoon."

"Why haven't you written me? Don't you remember? You said that we could make believe I am your sweetheart. You didn't even let me know you were coming home."

"In the cavalry, we get up at daybreak, ride and care for our horses, practice formations, and shoot weapons until dark. At night, we divide into teams and try to get as close to our opponents as possible without being seen or heard. We must clean our guns and wash clothes. Time simply runs out. I promise to do better."

"Get this straight." She shook her finger in his face. "If you don't write, I'll stop writing. Do you understand?"

"Yes, Mam." Jesse smiled. "You sound much older than you really are."

"How is Madge?"

"She is fine. Isn't it crazy for a grown man to carry a rag doll for good luck?"

"It isn't crazy to me." Her bright eyes searched his face. "Madge will keep you safe."

"Every morning, I look into her smiling face and smile back. I don't write often but I remember who made Madge."

BULL RUN'S FIRST BATTLE

THURSDAY/19. Company C boarded rail cars in Union City. William and Jesse led their horses from a boxcar in Richmond. Jesse said, "It's chilly tonight and look at all those stars. Do you realize we're only a hundred and ten miles from Washington?"

"Yeah. And I know Richmond, nestled here on the James River, is our capital. It is the North's primary objective. They capture Richmond and the war is over." William mounted his horse.

Rapidan River. Rivers played an important role

"Captain Perrin said that our main fortifications form a semi-circle north, east, and south of the city. In the morning we begin riding approximately 25 miles a day to identify our vantage points and mark them on maps."

At camp, they hitched their horses and bedded down on blankets.

FRIDAY/20. "MOUNT UP." Capt'n Perrin rode his white horse back and forth.

"That was a short night." Jesse tightened Sam's girth.

"Men. We're gonna ride until we see and hear the Yankees. We must know the lay of this land as well as we know the backs of our own hands. Frequently we shall dismount and hike through wooded areas, studying the terrain." Capt'n Perrin signaled silently with his hand.

OCTOBER, 1861

THURSDAY/17. After a hard week's ride Company C dismounted at Manassas. The men drank some water and sat on the ground.

The small stream, flowing beneath the famous "Stone Bridge",
named the "Battle of Bull Run."

"Yankees called this the Battle of Bull Run." Major W. E. Martin unfolded a large chart. "You are sitting on top of Henry Hill. After you've had a rest we'll ride down yonder to what is now the collapsed Stone Bridge, overlooking Bull Run. On Tuesday, 16, July, the Confederate Army clashed here with the Union Army. Those Yankees thought they'd come out here to this railroad junction, shoot at us, we'd tuck our tails and run like whipped dogs. That's not the way it was.

"Nearly everyone in Washington knew about the fight; so they lined the streets there and yelled for General McDowell's Army of thirty-five thousand. They marched out to begin the campaign which they would pursue until they captured Richmond and end the war.

That army was made up of young, green volunteers who came from all over. You should have seen their bright new uniforms. There wasn't a dirty spot on them. Not a man wanted to miss being in this mighty battle which would ensure a short war. Mercy sakes. Any thought of this being a one-sided war game ended with ten hours of barking rifles, roaring cannons, clanging steel, yelling Rebels, and gasping, dying men.

"Many congressmen thought this would be a sham battle, something like a good horse race. They told me the word spread throughout Washington that everybody who was somebody ought to pack lunches, bring wine, dress in their best clothes, ride their fancy carriages, and invite their women to watch an easy Yankee victory.

"What a surprise lay waiting on 18, July, McDowell's Army got to Centreville. That's just five miles north and east of here. This little winding stream, called 'Bull Run,' crossed the route which McDowell planned to travel.

"General Beauregard placed 22,000 Rebels to protect the fording places from Union Mills to Stone Bridge.

"McDowell tried moving to our right flank but we checked them over there at Blackburn's Ford. For the next two days our cavalry observed their scouting our left flank.

"Beauregard got in touch with Richmond to request help from General Joseph Johnston who commanded 10,000 troops stationed in the Shenandoah Valley.

"Using the Manassas Gap Railroad, General Johnston loaded most of his men onto cars and they reached our battle zone on 20 and 21st, July. Johnston outsmarted the Yankee forces. Many of our Rebel troops marched from the junction directly into battle.

"Let's ride east and a little north on this road. I'll show you something.

"Notice how Bull Run flows mostly south in front of us but about a mile and a quarter up there it turns a hard left; so it's flowing east for almost two miles. Our left flank formed back in here. At dusky day on the 21st, McDowell sent his attack columns toward Sudley Springs Ford. To distract us he ordered a diversionary attack on up this road to where Stone Bridge crosses Bull Run. At 5:30 we heard the bellow of a thirty pounder Parrot rifle which signaled the beginning.

"Our Colonel Nathan Evans commanded the troops at the Stone Bridge. McDowell's inexperienced troops sounded like a herd of buffaloes as they stumbled in the darkness. They tried to stay on those narrow roads as long as they could.

"Colonel Evans was a smart soldier. He realized the attack on our front was a diversion. He left a small force to hold the bridge and the rest of us hurried to Matthews Hill in time to confront McDowell's lead unit. Our force was too small to hold back the Yanks.

"Barnard Bee and Francis Bartow marched their brigades to assist us. Our lines gave way to the large number of Yankees and we high-tailed toward Henry Hill. General Thomas J. Jack's brigade arrived. Mounted on his horse over there on the rise of the hill, Jackson stood firm, assessing our predicament. Bee pointed to Jackson and shouted, 'There stands Jackson, like a stone wall. Rally behind the Virginians.'

General Barnard Bee pointed to Jackson, on a hill behind the fence,
and said, "There stands Jackson like a stone wall."

"General Beauregard, commander of the main force, and General Johnston arrived on Henry Hill. They calmed down our disorderly brigades.

"Violence and destruction stunned our young soldiers that morning. I believe the Yankees were stunned, too. They stopped advancing around noon.

"Having nearly an hour's lull in fighting, we reformed our lines in and along those trees at the foot of the hill. We needed to capture the Yanks' cannons along the crest of Henry Hill. Their booming frightened us more than they damaged.

"Mercy. Talk about a fight. Both sides, determined to force the other from the hill, fought man against man until after 4:00. To the south and west of Henry Hill, fresh Rebel units smashed into the Yankee's right flank. They call that 'Chinn Ridge.' Exhausted, McDowell's Army retreated.

I told you that Congressmen and many other dignitaries wanted to watch the Union Army defeat our Confederate Army. Folks in their fancy carriages congested the road to Washington. What began as an orderly Yankee retreat ended as a panicked rout. President Davis came on the field at the time our battle ended.

"We defeated the Union Army here but didn't follow through. By the morning of the 22nd, McDowell's Army was secure within the Washington defenses.

"Federals lost 2,708 men. We lost 1,982. The New York Herald released these figures."

FRIDAY/18. Company C pressed to Centreville under the command of Major W. T. Martin. They rode out to Camp Cooper, near General J. E. B. Stuart's headquarters. Jesse and William rode picket a mile east; a mile west.

While on picket and riding close to William, Jesse reined in Sam suddenly. "Look a yonder. There's a Yankee regiment coming up. They're setting up guns. Maybe we'll kill our first Yank."

"We've got to move closer." William dismounted and tethered his horse.

They crawled on their bellies to a bluff's edge. Jesse whispered. "It's the 20th Massachusetts. What are they shooting at? Company C is the only unit in this area and we're no where close to where they are firing. Let's move up stream and find out what's happening."

"Jesse." William pointed. "Look along the banks of the Potomac. Those Yanks are spooked by a colored funeral. I've never seen so many white handkerchiefs. Go back and tell Major Martin that the 20th is movin' up the river. I'll move with them and meet you at Edward's Ferry at daybreak.

"I'll stay with you until midnight. That'll give us time to see if any more troops move in."

Approximately two hours passed. Jesse and William inched to the edge of the Potomac's west bank. Jesse said, "They're beginning a night march. Let's get our horses."

"Have you got a compass? I left mine in our tent. At daylight I might need to know what direction they are traveling." William stopped. "I think I see a boat on the river."

"Yeah. In fact, I can see three. They're going to ferry those troops across right here. How can they move that many men in three boats? There's no need for you to follow them. Let's go."

"Major Martin. You remember that high wooded bluff over yonder on the river?" Jesse breathed deeply.

"Yeah. They call it Ball's Bluff." Major Martin curried his horse.

"Before dark William and I could read the 20th Massachusetts' flag. Later some other troops joined them. They're ferrying across the Potomac and it looks as if they're fanning out along some cow paths."

"Good work. I'll talk with General Stuart."

Jesse and William filled their canteens and fell in with Company C. They heard an excited voice coming from the river's edge. "Boys, you want to fight, don't you?"

"Yes, Sir." They shouted in unison.

"Move those guns. What's all the confusion? Move those guns. Now."

The Yanks couldn't detect Rebel cavalry and infantry forming in the thick woods.

In the dusky-day Major Martin watched a movement of gray coats. He ordered, "Load. FIRE,"

Company C moved closer. "Hold your fire. We shot at coats hanging in trees. Y'all did a great job of hitting your targets. It's' the 20th Massachusetts but where are the men?"

"There're two big guns to our right." A rebel voice screamed.

Infantry and cavalry, side by side, formed a line across the bluff. Firing commenced.

"You killed one." Jesse rammed powder into his barrel and put a cap in place. A big grin crossed his face. He mopped sweat.

"I wounded one what was aiming at Major Martin. I saw blood all over his right hand and up his sleeve." William mounted his horse.

"They're like ducks on a pond. They can't see us in this thicket. And we're on this high ground." Jesse mounted Sam.

"Watch Major Martin. I think we're fixin' to form a cavalry line and kill every Yankee in sight." William rode to Jesse and shook his hand.

"RRrrr, YEOW!!! The Rebels screamed as they charged. The 15th and 20th Massachusetts scrambled toward the river.

"Somebody must of hit a colonel or general, or something. Look at that crowd over yonder, totin' that soldier with a white plume in his hat." Jesse inched Sam down the hill.

"Watch out, Jesse. Yank on your left." A shot rang out. The Yankee's knees buckled.

"Good shot, William. The war could have been over for me." Jesse jumped off Sam and scooped a handful of the Yankee's blood. He dripped it over William's head. "I baptize you in the name of the Father, the Son, and the Holy Spirit."

Massive rifle fire erupted. Each breath inhaled black powder smoke. Men smashed into men. Horses tangled with horses. Bullets riddled the river water. Yanks poled their way on boats across the river.

Blood saturated the uniforms of two soldiers who held large poles. They fell against the gunwale, the boat tilted, and capsized. Thirty to forty men struggled and gurgled in the water until each drowned. Bottom-side-up, the boat drifted down stream. Darkness ate it.

FRIDAY/25. "Jesse and William take charge of the wounded. Medics will help y'all. To all you boys of Company C, I want you to know that I'm proud of your performance at Ball's Bluff. We took a few losses and some got wounded. We'll ride back to camp. Major Martin wants to review what happened here and we'll drill toward correctin' our mistakes." Captain Perrin saluted them.

"Water . . . Water. Oh God . . . Somebody give me a drink of water." A soldier lay, squeezing his mangled right leg.

"Get this boy on a stretcher." Jesse cradled the soldier in his arms. The canteen emptied.

"All right, you drivers. Form a train of ambulances. You wounded boys what can walk and sit up, load the first ambulance and move out. We're going to Warrenton Hospital. Fill the second, and so on." William handed a pair of crutches to a teenager.

"Hey, Taggart and Gandy. Help me with lifting this boy onto a stretcher." Jesse knelt on one knee. "Gently now. He's critical. Careful with that splint."

Their train of ambulances wove through ruts and stopped at Warrenton Hospital. Jesse and William supervised unloading the wounded and wrote personal data about each for the hospital.

They mounted their horses and returned to Company C. The company rode picket each day and took a scout occasionally.

ON TO MUNSON HILL

NOVEMBER, 1861

Saturday/23. "It's hard for me to realize today is 23, November, a mighty cold and blustery day." William salved his boot.

"Yeah. We could be home standing around a hot stove at Cooksville General Store. And Frank would be telling about the miracle of a dead deer he'd shot, getting up and running away. But we're in Virginia, freezing our tails off." Jesse placed a hand in his glove.

"FALL IN." Major Martin's voice boomed.

Fifty cavalrymen untethered their horses and mounted. "Boys, we'll ride to scout the area around Munson Hill. That's six miles northeast of Fairfax Courthouse, one and a half miles from Hunondoli, and the same from Falls Church."

At 12:00 noon, a rider pointed to a Yankee foraging party. Jesse said, "I believe they're about equal in number to us."

"Give me your attention." Major Martin stopped his horse. "Remember our drills. Work together, the way we practiced. CHARGE."

Jesse and William galloped their horses alongside each other. William said, "Just look how skilled this bunch of country boys has become."

"Yeah. It's great. READY? YEOW."

"Look at those Yankees turn tail. Spur ol' Sam" William grinned.

"They took flight" Jesse replaced his sword.

Major Martin rode around the circle of captured Yankees. Let's see now. We've got one sergeant, one captain, and 28 privates. Ain't that simply dandy? William, count up the other loot."

"Major, we got five wagons, 120 bushels of corn for our horses, 29 muskets, three repeaters, and 2 swords."

When they set up camp the following men signed the daily log: Pettus, A. M. Caskell, O. Kimbrough, N. Pickett, S. Vandevender, J. Creekmore, W. Daniel, J. Scarbrough, E. McDonald, Phelps, Turner N. Taggart, J. Gandy, C. Permenter, Y. Felton, S. Atkinson, and J. R. Sparkman.

SUNDAY/24. They rode from Camp Cooper and camped some 12 miles from Centreville.

FRIDAY/29. Jesse stood for inspection. He whispered to William, "I feel a fever."

"Are you a lily?"

"You know better'n that. I've got an achin' in my head and joints." He shook his arms.

"All right, boys." Major Martin frowned. "We have drill today. We'll ride to the outskirts of Centreville and confront a foe, wearing red armbands. Our job is to secure the north section of town. Any questions?"

DECEMBER, 1861

MONDAY/2. Jesse told William, "If I faint, just let me lay. This pain, all over, is awful."

At the end of that day, William walked into Major Martin's tent. "Sir, Jesse won't go to sick call. But he ain't no good to us the way he is. He must have104 fever."

TUESDAY/3. At daylight, Major Martin shouted, "FALL IN."

Jesse stood at attention. His body shivvered.

"Jesse, I command that you and William leave immediately for the Warrenton Hospital. After you check in, William will come on back. Dismissed."

"How'd he know I'm ailing?" Jesse packed a few belongings into his saddlebags.

"I reckon he saw you shaking." William mounted his horse and rode off.

They could see the hospital's grounds. William said, "Boy, this place is changing. It looks like a small village, just a buzzing. They've got shops of blacksmiths, shoe makers, carpenter shops, ice houses, commissaries, apothecaries, baggage masters, clerks, and quartermasters. Whatever you need, they've got."

"Paul, what's the matter with you?" Jesse looked at a bed.

"I'm getting over a case of the flu." Paul shook Jesse's hand. "The doctor is releasing me tomorrow; so I'll be going back to Company H. Even if you do look sick, it's sure good to see you. They'll take good care of you here and you'll be well in a few days. I'll see you again before I leave."

"Nurse, what day is this?" Jesse's voice sounded weak.

"5, December."

"I'm dying, aren't I?"

"William said to tell you that he's gone back to Company C. Take this medicine." The nurse poured a spoonful. "Here. Drink this glass of pure whiskey. Not everybody can have this stuff."

TUESDAY/10. Jesse walked from the hospital. He bridled Sam and turned to pick up his saddle. William hitched his horse. Jesse said, "I thought you were with the company."

"I was but I caught what you had."

"Do you want me to stay with you? I feel much better, and I thank you for making me come." Jesse dropped his saddle.

"Naw. You need the drills."

"It's just four days until Christmas and here we are in sight of Mount Vernon, riding formation. I miss William but I'm glad you and I have this chance to ride together."

"William's been sick for two weeks." Caskell spurred his horse. "And look over yonder. There's Mount Vernon. We're mighty close to Washington and Yanks will be thick as flies. They're gonna shoot first; then ask who we were."

"How'd you like to rock on a big front porch such as that?"

"I'd rather be in Miss'ippi."

"Do you reckon the Potomac is about three miles wide here?"

Jesse's eyes squinted.

"More'n that."

"Company, HALT." Major Martin ordered. "Dismount and rest for fifteen minutes."

Jesse and several others led their horses to the Potomac's bank. While the horses drank Jesse said, "I told Caskell the river is three miles across. What do y'all think?"

He guessed five miles, another four, one three and a half.

"All right. Let's settle on four. We need some of those smart engineers with us. They could tell us exactly how many pontoons it'd take to cross it." Jesse walked back up the hill.

WEDNESDAY/25. "Merry Christmas, Caskell. Major Martin said that we'd spend today in and around this camp." Jesse gathered some wood. He started a small fire.

"This is my first Christmas away from home." Caskell added some sticks to the fire. "I miss the Christmas decorations and the smell of fruit cake with a little whiskey over it."

"Yeah, And I miss all the Sparkmans gathering around big log fires to swap gifts and talk about crops and all the kin folks. An' lie about who killed the biggest deer." Jesse stared into the flames.

"The cooks are going to serve some eggnog after we eat dinner. Some of our scouts raided a turkey yard last night; so the cooks are fixing that with sweet potatoes."

"Well. That's like home." While Jesse soaked a uniform in hot, soapy water, he addressed an envelope to his parents. He placed a stub of a pencil into his coat pocket and felt Madge. "I've got to write Sallie, too."

"Who's Sallie?" Caskell smiled.

"She's my sweetheart and we're going to get married after the war." He unfolded some crumpled up paper. "I heard somebody say that we might get mail tomorrow."

"You probably know that I ain't learned to read and write yet. Would you mind writing to my folks?"

"I'd enjoy that."

"Jesse. It's 9:30. I want you and Caskell to ride a scout today. Go down the river for an hour. Break. And come back in. Eat dinner and then ride toward Washington." Major Martin wrote in his log.

"Major, I'm fixin' to write a letter for Caskell's folks."

"Mail's not going out until tomorrow." Major rode away. He stopped and turned his horse around. "Oh. You remember seeing all the Yankees carrying the man with the white plume at Ball's Bluff. We received word that one of our cavalry shot through the heart of a Colonel Baker. He was a politician from Oregon and a close friend of President Lincoln."

"Great." Jesse waved his cap.

"This is a Christmas to remember. But we're lucky that no Yanks shot at us." Caskell unsaddled his horse and walked toward smoking embers of their fire.

"It'll be dark real soon. Let's find some wood and get our fire going. I feel the pangs of camp fever again. I can't throw it off."

"The medics have some new medicine. Go see him in the morning." Caskell blew into the coals and a small flame ignited.

WINTER QUARTERS

JANUARY, 1862

W EDNESDAY/1. Before daybreak, Jesse heard his tent shudder. He reached for his musket.

"HAPPY NEW YEAR, JESSE. Wake up. It's 1862. I'm home. Aren't you glad to see me?" William Daniel grabbed Jesse's warm foot.

"Get your cold hand away from my foot, you dope." Jesse threw back his blanket. He stood outside their tent and shivvered as he buttoned the drop-seat of his long underwear. "Sure, I'm glad to see you but I could break your neck for waking me up."

"Boy. I had a miserable ride all night. It's freezing cold and there's a drizzle of some sort."

"How are you?" Jesse pulled his coat collar higher.

"I'm a new man. You've got to meet the pretty nurse I had."

"We've been riding our tails off and you've been enjoying the company of a gorgeous nurse for three weeks. You got here in time to ride back through Warrenton. We're going that way to reach the Confederate winter quarters near Centreville."

"She even falsified my temperature." William drank from his canteen.

Jesse and William rode beside each other in company formation. Negroes swarmed Warrenton's streets. Some staggered into the cavalry's route. Jesse yelled to one, "What're you doing here, Boy?"

"I'se come to be hired out."

"You better be careful or some soldier will ride over you."

"They ain't got no right to do that. Washington is just a little piece from here. President Lincoln will have his neck."

"Don't count on that." Jesse yelled back.

Company C rode into camp near Centreville. William said, "Looks as if we've got work to do. Whoever told us this place is ready for winter quarters gave us some bad information."

"That area over yonder on the hill looks good." Jesse's eyes sparkled.

"Yeah, but Major Martin is signaling for us to stop here."

"Boys, We'll be here in winter quarters for approximately six weeks." Major Martin read the names of men who would room together. William Daniel, M. Fink, William Garner, J. B. May, and Jesse Sparkman. Go to the supply depot over yonder and on the bulletin board you'll find a set of plans for building a log cabin. Check out tools from the quartermaster and he will tell you about the logs. The better you build your cabin, the better winter you'll have."

"Stop riding this saw. You know that two can play your game." Jesse let go his end of the cross-cut saw.

After the saw bowed nearly double, William lay sprawled on the ground. He laughed. "I told you, back in Scooba, you'd have to be tough to stay up with me."

"You might fool J. B. into letting you ride the saw but I've been raised up pulling my share. Jesse rolled up his sleeves. "It doesn't take much of this to turn a winter day into summer."

"Hey, Garner. Do you know how to cut out these notches with an axe?" William rested.

"Yeah. When you and Jesse need a relief from sawing, me and Finck are handy. J. B. is an expert with a hatchet. He can make our shingles."

A cold drizzle peppered them. After a while the wet logs clogged the saw teeth. Wet axe handles slowed their notching logs to fit. They placed coats over their dampened uniforms.

TUESDAY/14. William Daniel started home.

Nights followed days and days faded into nights, until the log cabin provided shelter for them. They moved in and slept on hard bunks, softened with straw. The cabin was damp and cold. A. P. Sparkman moved in with them for a week.

They were marching on the drill field when Jesse whispered. "This icy wind is cutting to my bones."

"The medic gave me some olive oil to rub on my legs where the saddle wore off the skin. They're raw . . . . Look like raw beef steak." A. P. got in step.

"Company HALT. LEFT. FACE." Major Martin stood at the center of the company. "Boys. We will drill an hour each morning and afternoon. Right now, Captain Perrin and I will demonstrate hand-to-hand combat. And then y'all pair off and practice what we teach you."

A.P. simulated jabbing a bayonet through Jesse's stomach. With a dagger Jesse simulated slitting A. P.'s throat.

"All right. That's enough of that. When we dismiss go and saddle up your horses. You are to exercise them each day for one hour after drill. "FALL OUT."

THURSDAY/16. Jesse left camp, which is three miles from Camp Clifford. Miserable weather set-in.

FRIDAY/17. Major Martin shouted to the formation. "You boys let that red company run over you today. Ninety percent casualty. Y'all have got to stay low and use the cover of brush piles, rocks, and tree stumps. If you are on horseback, protect each other. Make those horses lay down. It's better to lose a horse than a man."

TUESDAY/28. S. T. Atkinson and J. H. Fraley died. Jesse said, "This miserable weather won't let up. Men and horses are dying."

FEBRUARY, 1862

SATURDAY/1. After being paid, Finck said, "I've got a deck of cards. Anybody interested in a friendly little game of chance? Come to our cabin after drill."

"I've got almost a dollar in change I'll invest. A. P. Sparkman dug into his pocket.

William Garner said, "I've got a couple of dollars."

Five boys got down on their knees in front of the cabin and placed varying amounts of money on the ground. Finck said, "We'll cut for high card to see who deals and the dealer names the game."

Just before dark, Jesse looked into the eyes of each player and smiled. "This is my last hand. I've lost my dollar."

He watched six boys win and lose, back and forth, until darkness ended the game. He said, "I know that we are fearful of an angry God. We'll have to discard these instruments of sin before battle."

"But we can play for fun until we break camp." A. P. counted almost four dollars worth of change. "Jesse, I'll challenge you to a wrestling match tomorrow, at the south end of our drill field."

"I'll take that and bet two dollars that I pin your shoulders to the ground two out of three times."

"The medic weighed me at 192 pounds yesterday. How much did you weigh?" A. P. flexed his arms.

"I'm 189. That's close enough."

SUNDAY/2. Company C formed a large circle. "All right, Boys." Major Martin smiled. "There'll be no bitin', stickin' fingers in the eyes, nor kickin' one another in the groins. Strip down to your waists and get after each other."

"Look out, Jesse. I told you you'd have to be tough to keep up with me." A. P. tightened his arm around Jesse's neck.

Jesse placed his thumb beneath A. P.'s jaw-bone and pressed upward. A. P.'s head moved up and back. Jesse positioned his right leg behind A. P.'s knees and 381 pounds of solid muscle hit the ground.

"Ooooo." Faces squinched.

A.P. rolled on top and pinned Jesse's shoulders to the ground.

"One—two—three—four—five." That's a win for A. P."

Jesse faked a grab for A. P.'s arms. Instead he grasped the right hand and A. P. moaned as he bent to his knees. Jesse locked his legs around A. P.'s waist and squeezed. A. P. gulped, "I can't breathe."

"I know. Put your shoulders on the ground."

A.P. tried to wrench his body from the vice, only to feel Jesse's legs tighten. A. P. grimaced and squared his shoulders on the ground.

"One—two—three—four—five. That's one each." Major Martin shouted.

Jesse passed through A. P.'s outstretched arms. Jesse's arms locked in the middle of A. P.'s back. Jesse planted both feet and pushed. A P. fell backwards and his shoulders never moved from the ground.

"And the winner is, Jesse Sparkman." Major lifted Jesse's arm.

"I been sick," A. P. smiled and shook Jesse's hand.

"I'll beat you next time."

"You know good and well that I lucked out on you but give the money to me anyway."

Pettus said, "I enjoyed y'all's wrestling match. Earlier, I went by the Quartermaster's and he saved six nail kegs for us. Come with me and each of us can carry two. Maybe we can get some paint to brighten them up."

"You're a great home maker, Pettus." A. P. placed an arm around his shoulders.

"I see that some of the boys cut logs and stood them on end for stools. Some used wooden boxes, and they double for storage." Jesse looked from cabin to cabin. "I predict this Jeff Davis' Legion will win many battles. The spirit is higher'n a kite.

"If you want to learn how to win wars play chess. I have a chess set and maybe the Quartermaster will give us some boards that we can paint a checkerboard on." Pettus blew warm air into his palms and rubbed them together.

"Look at your breath. The weather is turning colder." Jesse put on a pair of dark gloves.

"I remember you. Yeah. I remember you." The Quartermaster smiled and pointed to Jesse. "I learned not to tease boys about their good luck charms. I had a terrible headache when I came to."

"Excuse me for losing my temper. It had been a long day. The three of us are working on ways to break the monotony of camp life. We keep doing the same things over and over, every day. Do you have some boards from wooden boxes that you are going to burn or throw away? We want to make a checkerboard."

"Yeah. Look behind this warehouse."

Jesse and Pettus placed several small boards into their nail kegs. A. P. checked out a hammer, square, and an assortment of nails. The Quartermaster said, "Take a bunch of those feed sacks. Y'all can have sack races."

"Good idea." A. P. stuffed sacks into his kegs.

Jesse whittled on a long thin board while Pettus and A. P. sawed, hammered, and nailed. After a while an instrument resembling a sword lay on the ground. Jesse closed his knife. "I'll challenge anybody to a sword fight."

"I'll take that challenge." Pettus selected a board and traced Jesse's sword. "It's nearly dark now but I'll finish my sword and meet you at the drill field tomorrow at 4:30."

"We can dual right here in our own front yard." Jesse picked up his sword.

"Mail call for Company C." Major Martin opened a bag. "Look at this pretty package. Hmnn. "It smells real sweet. Let's see. In the upper left hand corner it says, 'From Sallie Denton, Geiger, Alabama. Oh. And it's sealed with LOVE. To Jesse Sparkman."

Jesse grinned and tore the wrapping paper off. He held up a pair of woolen, hand-made socks. He sat on the ground and kicked off his boots. Men laughed as he wiggled bare toes, emerging from his old socks.

"Major, you've been pushing us too hard. This is the best pair of socks I've got." Jesse replaced his boots and walked about. "This is like walking on air."

FRIDAY/7. Jesse mounted Sam. They fell into formation with Company C.

SUNDAY/9. They reached Warrenton. Jesse's eyes scanned Main Street. "This place is looking better. It's one of the finest I know of for summer but mercy sakes, it's cold right now. We've got to find a convenient place and build a fire."

"Do you get the feeling that our boys are getting over excited because we expect the Yanks at any time now?" A. P. stacked some wood.

"I suspect they're scared 'cause they saw what happened to the Yanks we shot when we were at Munson Hill. There's a heap of difference between drilling and actually killing a man. You know, yourself, how that screaming got to you. A man doesn't scream except for torture."

"Yeah. And you keep talking about smelling the innards from their blown open stomachs."

"Boy. That's a slow dying."

McCLELLAN'S PENINSULA CAMPAIGN

WEDNESDAY/12 Company C rode into Culpeper, Virginia.

THURSDAY/13. They boarded cars heading to Gordonsville. Jesse squeezed A. P.'s knee. "I feel sick to my stomach."

"Wake up, Jesse. Can you hear me?" A. P. looked into the aisle. "You passed out. Your eyes are glassy."

In Gordonsville, the doctor beamed a candle light into Jesse's eyes. "Chimborazo Hospital in Richmond is the largest ever built in the western hemisphere. It covers a high hill near the city's west boundary. I can send you over there."

"I feel fine, Doctor. I think I had motion sickness. I was looking out the train window, watching everything whiz by, when I went blank."

"There's talk about lettin' women work there. I don't believe women have any business in a hospital where men are lying all over the place and many of them covered only with sheets or blankets."

"They have women at Warrenton." Jesse tightened his belt.

"It ain't right. Open your mouth and say 'ah.' I'm gonna give you some medicine and send you back to your company."

Jesse and A. P. rode back into camp that night. A. P. said, "While I waited for the doctor to look at you I read a newspaper. General George McClellan of the Union Army equipped and marched an army of 130,000, but they didn't go anywhere. The paper said that President Lincoln forced The Army of the Potomac to make a move."

"Look out, Richmond, Here they come" Jesse stretched out on his bunk. "Major Martin told some of us that General Stuart has organized us into the best cavalry there is, and the Yanks are scared of us."

"We can find out more from the newspapers than we can from our officers. General McClellan concluded from scouting reports that General Joseph Johnston is outnumbered two to one at Manassas. McClellan devised an oblique drive on Richmond."

"What's oblique?"

"I think it means a slanted movement. You know how we form lines and move straight into our targets?"

"Yeah."

"If you look at a map you can see that the Virginia Peninsula forms between the James and York Rivers. The best I can tell, General McClellan plans to transfer his Army of the Potomac down the peninsula. General McDowell's Federal Corps, located at Fredericksburg, will move down and support McClellan. McClellan will move westward and upward. Their navy made the news, too."

"What do you mean?"

"While the Army of the Potomac moves upward the navy will steam up the James River and protect their left flank. All this mass of trained force will attack and capture Richmond."

Jesse said, "It's hard for us to know what our navy is doing when we don't come in direct contact with it. It transports essential food and ammunition to supply depots along the coasts and rivers. Early in the war Confederates captured their Merrimac and converted it into an ironclad. Now we call it 'The Virginia.'"

MARCH, 1862

"The Yankees came out with an updated ironclad, The Monitor. Some of the experts say that it looks like a tin can on a shingle. Would you want to ride a boat?" A. P. smiled.

"I got seasick riding a train."

TUESDAY/18. E. McDonald came back to Culpeper for Jesse. They put out on foot, hiking cross-country for Company C. McDonald said, "I guess you heard what happened at Hampton Roads on 9, March."

"No."

"The Federals tested their Monitor against our Virginia. They steamed, belched smoke, fired volleys of ammunition, and banged into each other for three hours. The Virginia has ten guns and a battering ram but The Monitor maneuvered circles around her. If the Virginia had won we would control the Chesapeake Bay. But due to a draw, General McClellan put his grand Peninsular Campaign into action."

"We'll probably ride in that direction real soon." They walked into Camp Benton nine miles from Madison Courthouse.

A.P. shook hands with Jesse. "This is fine living. My belly is full. Look at this new uniform from cap to boots. I've been feedin' Sam and he can almost pull a freight train."

"I'm ready for a new uniform." Jesse tossed his bag into their shelter.

SATURDAY/29. At daybreak heavy clouds hovered over camp. Major Martin formed the company and held up a piece of paper. "Boys, we'll ride diagonally into this biting north wind today. General Johnston ordered us to the Rappahanock River. Mount up. Close order. March."

"Snow hit me in the face. Have you felt any?" Jesse placed a chew of tobacco into his mouth.

"Yeah."

"We've been riding at close order almost two hours. I see a little church up yonder. Stop your horses there and let them rest." Major Martin galloped to the rear of the company.

"These sausage biscuits and coffee make a good breakfast." Jesse emptied his cup.

A.P. wiped more than an inch of snow from his saddle and mounted. Jesse and Sam fell in beside him. A. P. said, "The snow is so thick it's almost blinding. I hope I don't ride over anybody."

"I wish you could see your face. Your beard is ice-caked and looks like a white mask. Mercy. You're ugly." Jesse laughed.

"You're not the most handsome soldier in the cavalry. Sam's mane and tail are frozen." A. P. broke an icy hair from Sam.

Before dark the snow changed to sleet; then rain. Major said, "Boys, we'll stop in these woods for the night. The trees should protect us some from this bone-cutting wind."

Jesse propped against a large tree trunk. He wrapped a blanket over his head and shoulders.

Water oozed into his gloves. Ice crackled whenever he adjusted the blanket.

SUNDAY/30. At daylight Jesse listened to A. P.'s teeth chatter.

"Wake up, A. P. Let's wrestle to get our circulation going." Gently, Jesse slapped A. P.'s face and pounded his back.

"It can't be time to ride."

Chilling rain continued. They saddled up their horses. Water dripped from stirrups.

"Ride. Ride we must, Boys, to reach the Rappahanock." Major Martin led the company north and easterly.

After dark Company C stopped riding, within two miles of the river. Jesse said, "My legs ache slam down to my toes."

"I'm exhausted." A. P. stretched his arms. "I'm hungry but there's no food to eat."

"Boys, I know you're wet, cold, and hungry. Maybe tomorrow will be better." Major Martin tightened his collar.

MONDAY/31. Morning clouds began breaking up; sunbeams reached down. Men built fires, warmed their bodies and dried uniforms. That evening they bedded down dry but hungry.

"You know, William." Jesse placed a log on their fire. "This isn't a neat, crystal-clear fight against a foreign country. We're fighting other states, men who have different beliefs than ours. Right now I'd be happy just to eat one piece of bread."

"Yeah. I heard rumors about civilian politicians and military leaders in Washington who don't trust each other. We've got the Yankees confused and scared of us. That's good."

"General Joe Johnston pulled off a real fooler on the Yanks today. I believe I got more black paint on me than I did on those small logs." Jesse rubbed paint with a kerosene soaked rag.

"The general selected strategic positions along the Rappahanock for us to place axles of wagon wheels. Company H took the black logs and centered them between the wheels. At a distance they looked exactly like cannons guarding the river."

"I was out riding a picket today. Virginia Cavalry reconnaissance reports indicated that General McClellan's Army outnumbered the Rebels' three to one." A. P. removed his boots and wiggled his toes.

"With y'all's innocent logs guarding the river General Johnston's orders came down. 'Move your army from the trenches and march to points behind the river.'"

Major Martin said, "General Johnston ordered that our supply depots near Centreville and Manassas be burned and they went up in black smoke. Someone estimated a million pounds of bacon burned."

"Boy. We could have eaten well with that." Jesse patted his stomach.

"You're right. But we couldn't get to it." Major Martin picked up a stick and drew in the dirt. The fire flickered. "Our army evacuated batteries along the Potomac; as we can't clearly see what's going on in the area surrounding Washington. But, our empty spaces at Manassas confused the Union chess player."

"McClellan has poised his grand army on the Peninsula tip. To hasten protection of Richmond General Johnston has moved there, too."

APRIL, 1862

TUESDAY/1. With the whole army formed in line of battle, Jesse thought: Where are the Yankees?

We've been here all day. Hours seem like days. Oh, well. It's a beautiful Spring day.

Scouting reports said that General McClellan planned to float his army to the mouth of the Rappahanock and land at Urbanna. That would put him to General Johnston's rear but Johnston moved.

With very little food Company C rode beside the Rappahanock.

FRIDAY/4. Jesse said, "I got hold of some cornbread from a little boy who fished in the river."

While camped at Kellis' Mill the cavalry got six crackers a day. A cavalry picket described what he saw and concluded about the Army of the Potomac. "I looked from a woods north of Cumberland Landing on the Pamunky River. A blacksmith's shop mounted on a wagon was the closest thing to me. The blacksmith attached his anvil to a keg of horseshoe nails. He stored hammers, rasps, stoppers and pullers in a tool box on the rear. His furnace, with bellows, was in a fire-brick box.

Not very far to the south of the blacksmith, horses stood hitched for shoeing. Men hitched teams to supply wagons and ambulances as fast as they could. Cooks near the provisions prepared their fires while General McClellan inspected the Union troops. Thousands upon thousands of infantry assembled. As far as I could see tents lined the edge of the woods south of me. They didn't stack their rifles but took them to formation for inspection. Their horses and mules appeared to a mite underfed.

"From where I was, their rifles looked new but they were those ol' sorry smooth-bore makes that will hardly shoot across the Rappahanock."

MONDAY/7. Just before daybreak Jesse heard pitter-patter of sleet on his tent. He wrapped up in his blanket but heard the call to mount-up. He rode a scout almost twelve miles to the river. He searched for Yankees all day, peering into the haze and slipping on hardened sleet. No Yanks.

TUESDAY/8. "Mount-up." Major Martin ordered while snow fell onto the frozen ground.

"Surely the purpose of this ride is for us to return to camp." Jesse fell in beside A. P.

They rode hard until 11:00 P. M. Snow continued falling, wind cut into their exposed flesh, many faces turned a near purple, and tags of ice dangled from men's whiskers. Jesse and A. P. found some rails and built a fire. They placed their hands at the edge of the fire to thaw.

WEDNESDAY/9. Jesse laughed. "Henry fell asleep on top of three rails and slept all night."

Riding in formation Company C passed near Rapidan Station. Riders with pack mules met them and took wagons to camp. After reaching camp Jesse joined the line formed in front of the portable kitchen. A muddy soldier said, "Oh God, we're thankful for a warm supper. Let it go well with us. Amen."

Jesse gathered a bundle of straw and made it into a bed. Sam ate a small bucket of mixed feed.

THURSDAY/10. Is it morning already? The sun is rising beautifully for the first time in days." Jesse nudged A. P. "Did you hear me?"

FRIDAY/11. "Mount-up." Major Martin pointed his horse in a southerly direction. "Boys. We're gonna ride toward Richmond. Today will be a long one. HEAD 'EM OUT."

They rode all day.

SATURDAY/12. Late in the afternoon, at Louisa Courthouse, they met with fifty Legion men. Major announced, "Bed down here for the night. We received word that McClellan's Army of the Potomac wants to fight with us. What do y'all say?"

"Bring 'em on." Came a unified shout.

"The paper said that President Lincoln requested General McClellan come to Washington and meet in the White House. There's immense concern about the Peninsula Campaign. It will take their huge army into our familiar ground where they said, 'that vicious, blood-thirsty cavalry may strike its lethal blow without warning.'"

Jesse said, "I found a Richmond paper in Rapidan Station. President Lincoln, who has very little knowledge in military affairs and his cabinet are suspicious of General McClellan. The word which the president hesitated to say finally came out, 'treason.'

"Someone advised the cabinet, confidentially, that General McClellan planned on leaving the Capitol unprotected and we Rebels could take over easily. The general told them that the words cut to the quick and demanded President Lincoln to take back his statement. General McClellan stormed about the room and then walked out."

Major Martin said, "Our scouts told General Joe Johnston that the cabinet wants the Army of the Potomac to march straight down the railroad. Perhaps you boys know that McClellan is commander of the entire Union forces and thinks he is the Chosen One to win the war. He plans to coerce the Southern States into a life of submission and bow to the demands of Northerners."

"We're gonna change his plans." A. P. ate a cracker and washed it down with water.

SUNDAY/13. Company C continued a southerly route. Jesse said, "This is the same road we passed over when we rode from Richmond to Manassas. See, there're the outskirts of Richmond."

Inside the city limits Pettus said, "Look at those young ladies poised along the sidewalks and all we can do for them is wave. Wave Jesse, wave."

"I'm waving. Look to our left."

Company C camped eight miles east of Richmond. Jesse and Pettus built a small fire. William Daniel returned from furlough.

WEDNESDAY/16. The First Virginia Cavalry joined the Jeff Davis Legion and marched for Yorktown.

"I saw little Sallie Denton when I went to church at Cooksville." William adjusted the girth on his horse. "The truth is she saw me and when church let out she ran up to me. She wanted to know where you were."

"She's twelve years old now. I wrote a birthday letter to her in February." Jesse reached into his saddle bag. "I received six letters from her yesterday. She wrote that it's spring-time all over Miss'ippi and Alabama. Leaves and grass are growing tall."

"I've got a gut feeling that we're fixing to fight a big war. Sallie said that you'd been good about writing. She's beginning to look like a young lady. Pretty eyes and a slender body."

FRIDAY/25. Jesse looked at the James River. "Across yonder is Yorktown. Williamsburg is five miles west of us. We're joining General Johnston's retreating army."

Major Martin said, "We successfully stalled the Army of the Potomac by entrenching from Yorktown to the James River. Some of McClellan's scouts reported and patrols verified that we evacuated our trenches; so he began moving up the peninsula."

"He must have got a real shocker." William grinned. "He didn't find wooden cannons, such as we decoyed at Manassas."

"Reckon what he thought when he realized those were real cannons pointing at his army?" Jesse bit a chaw of tobacco. "It's a shame we had to leave those Navy cannons, because they were too heavy to drag through all that mud."

"Those cannons won't do the Yanks any good. They're having hard enough time finding any high ground out of the mire of mud." Major Martin mounted his horse.

"What time you got, Major?"

"Eleven o'clock."

"Yanks marching in line." A picket galloped into camp. A few shots from skirmishers rang out. Company C fell back. Marching less than a mile, Major Martin discovered his company cut off by the Yanks. The Yankees came up to Company C's front and fired cannon over the column.

"Company C. Right about WHEEL." Major Martin shouted.

Arriving at the river's edge, Jesse's eyes darted here and there. "There's a Yankee boat. No. No. It's Rebel."

Rebel infantry and artillery covered Company C while they made good their escape. Occasionally during the night Yank pickets fired their guns.

MAY, 1862

MONDAY/5. In the breaking dawn a Rebel picket's horse galloped into camp. "Yankee skirmishers on our right."

"MOUNT UP." Major Martin's voice rang clearly.

"CHARGE."

Jesse fired, reloaded, fired six more rounds. A Yankee loaded and aimed his musket within a horse-length.

Sam galloped in a circle. Jesse felt his wrist absorb a shock. His sword pierced the Yankee's heart. He heard the squish as his sword sucked flesh around it, coming out.

"Jesse, cover me while I reload." William's eyes glared.

"Duck" Jesse shot a Yankee who was riding behind William.

"We're even. Now, we've got to fight our way back to the company." William rode his bay next to Sam. "Thanks."

"Look at the smoke from this point-blank fight. Stay side by side. We've got to risk it right through their middle. "YE HOO!!" Jesse spurred Sam.

Their horses trampled over soldiers. The main body of Company C formed in line of battle.

"FALL BACK." Major Martin turned his horse around.

Near the river they rode into a wooded area. "All right, Boys. That fight was a desperate one. Y'all did great. It's eleven o'clock now. We'll ride by the ammunition wagons and replenish. At three o'clock we're gonna charge their infantry in front of Fort Magruder. We'll charge; then fall back. Stay together the best you can."

Major Martin. Look to your left. There's the Second Florida Regiment." Jesse rode alongside.

"We'll join them and commence the fight." He made a silent signal with his right hand and Company C fell in line of battle.

"Boy. This Yankee infantry is hard and fierce. Have you seen their flag?" Jesse poured black powder from his horn.

"Haven't looked for it."

"What happened to your pants?"

"A Yank locked his arms around my leg and tried to pull me off. I cut his throat. He hung on for a while and I drug him a little ways." William gulped water from his canteen.

"Major Martin signaled for us to assemble."

"Boys. It's mighty near dark now. We're gonna tether our horses and fight the Yanks. Shoot them if you can. Kill them with bayonets, daggers, or choke them to death. Anything.

"Dismount. Six boys guard our horses. Wedge formation. Let's go. Let's go."

Battle raged.

"Retreat. With Vigor, RETREAT. Rally around the Second Florida. It's after midnight. Keep that noise down."

"It's great to see the sun come up. Looks as if the whole Rebel Army is here." Jesse placed a piece of cheese between two crackers.

"Yeah. Our army is to fall back in good order and we're to protect the rear. Word came down from headquarters that General Jackson left General Ewell in General Bank's front. Jackson marched up the Shenandoah Valley and routed General Robert Milroy's forces. Lend me a piece of cheese." William smiled.

Jesse cut off a slice of cheese and licked his knife. "Want more?"

"You might charge me interest."

"We need to get back to the Chickahominy. It's eighteen miles."

"Our problem is 100,000 Yankees." William mounted his bay.

SUNDAY/18. Company C stopped at the river's edge. Jesse said, "We must have left our horses saddled for eight solid days. Ol' Sam got cut by a few swords."

"I haven't had a bite to eat for two days. I fixed a pair of suspenders from a feed sack, 'cause my pants dropped over my 'hind end.'" William pitched a handful of dewberries into his mouth.

"Look who are riding into camp. There come Dempsey and your brother, John." Jesse pointed toward the road.

"Hey. Y'all missed the action. Have you got anything to eat with you?" William shook their hands.

"We've got some hard tack in our saddle bags. John dismounted and opened his bag.

"Y'all don't know what hungry is. We ran out of food and the Yanks stayed between us and supply." Jesse ate his berries and bread.

TUESDAY/20. Major Martin ordered, "MOUNT UP."

"I don't know about you but I feel great." Jesse looked at William.

"Those two days eased the pressure. Probably, I've gained five pounds and our horses got good care." William pulled a piece of tobacco from his shirt pocket.

"Sam has a new set of shoes and a full belly. The Chickahominy is really pretty today. How far do you reckon we are from Richmond?"

"My guess is we're about eight miles above and east of her."

"HALT." Major Martin stopped his horse. "Mechanicsville is two miles that way. We'll set up camp here. Count off and every fourth man can ride into town tonight. There'll be bed-check at 11:00."

FRIDAY/23. Shots rang out early. A voice shouted. "Yanks attacking our pickets."

"Form a line." Major waved his sword. "Forward. MARCH. FIRE."

Jesse fired to his left. Reloaded. He continued a brisk firing for several hours. Gimme some ammunition."

"I'm out. Let's high-tail it back to the wagons." William spurred his horse.

At the wagons Quartermaster said, "General Stonewall Jackson's brigades struck the heart of General Banks' retreating columns up north and west of here, at Front Royal. A fast moving fight forced the Yankees through Winchester. And later Banks moved across the Potomac."

SUNDAY/25. Company C rode out from Mechanicsville and assembled with the troops. Confederate baggage wagons replenished dwindling supplies of food and ammunition.

"Let me have your attention." Major Martin cleared his throat. "While we're camped here we'll elect officers and decide company duty."

"I nominate Jesse Sparkman for First Lieutenant." William waved to Major Martin.

"Any other nominations." Major looked over the company. Silence.

"Congratulations. Lieutenant. Boys. We can't ever let down. General Stonewall Jackson gave his troops a rest as a reward for their recent victory.

They narrowly escaped being captured by a convergence of Yank forces. General McDowell's Corps moved in from Fredericksburg. General John Fremont's Army marched from the west and General Banks re-crossed the Potomac."

A rider trotted into camp. "Mount up for picket, Sir."

SEVEN PINES

SATURDAY/31. Rebels followed General Joe Johnston and attacked Yanks at Seven Pines. Nine miles south and east of Richmond, on the Williamsburg road, Company C formed their station on the right flank. Major Martin ordered, "CHARGE."

Hoofbeats rumbled the earth. Yankee cannon and muskets shocked the Rebels. Battle raged very hot all day.

"There's enough daylight to see. Don't fire until you see the white of their eyes. Any questions?" Major's eyes scanned the troops.

"You want us to shoot out brown or blue eyeballs?" William smiled.

"All eyeballs."

Fighting let up. Jesse's boys guarded many Yank prisoners. Onto wagons they loaded weapons and ammunition. Jesse told them, "We'll move back to Mechanicsville and camp."

JUNE, 1862

WEDNESDAY/11. Jesse's boys lay idle in camp, Major Martin reported, "Got good news. General Jackson retreated through Harrisonburg on 8, June. Surprisingly, suddenly he turned and attacked the Yanks. General Ewell's division inflicted heavy defeat on General Fremont's troops at Cross Keys. And, on 9, June, General Jackson assaulted General James Shields' division of McDowell's Corps at Port Republic. That's south and east of Harrisonburg. By sunset that day three battered Yank armies got shoved out of the Shenandoah Valley."

Jesse packed three day's rations of hard bread and bacon. He mounted Sam and rode toward Ashland. During the noon hour he joined General Jeb Stuart who studied his entire command here. "Lieutenant Sparkman, it's almost sunset and Lieutenant Timberlake is more familiar with this territory than you. Take your boys and scout the Yank's positions. Report back to me before midnight."

"Yes, Sir." Jesse saluted. His boys rode until after nine o'clock without making a discovery. Jesse tethered Sam to a hitching rack in front of a six-column mansion. Tap, tap, tap of his heels echoed in the night's stillness. An elderly lady peeked from a window.

"Mam, I hate to bother you at this time of night but have you seen any Yanks pass this way?"

"You're nearly an hour behind a large number of soldiers. They took our chickens from the hen-house and rode east when they left."

"Thank you, Mam." Jesse turned and hurried down the steps.

"Sergeant, ride back to headquarters and tell General Stuart that we won't be back by midnight because we're tracking some Yanks headed east."

Standing on the porch the lady said, "We made fresh buttermilk today. Would you boys like some cornbread and milk?"

"Yes, Mam." Seven boys bunched up around her kitchen table.

"We hate to eat an' run, Mam, but we've got to find those Yankees." Jesse gulped down his milk. "You've been more than generous."

Small campfires dotted a wooded area. Lieutenant Timberlake said, "Jesse, I'll take five men into the Yank's lines while you cover us."

"All right. Make notes the best you can and we'll decipher them at day break."

FRIDAY/13. Headquarter's clock showed 2:15. Jesse told his boys, "Get as much rest as you can before seven."

With fifteen cavalrymen he rode for Hanover Courthouse. "Look. There are some two hundred Yanks. Considering their numbers we'll politely give them the road. Let's scamper into the woods here and hope they didn't see us."

Yanks marched by while Jesse's boys poised in the undergrowth. "That's a relief. We'll join a column of riders. We'll ride scout back and forth between the Pamonkey and Chickahominy Rivers." Jesse wiped sweat from his forehead.

At 2:05 P.M., a voice whispered, "There're the Yanks' pickets."

"CHARGE." Jesse shouted and Sam leaped ahead of the other horses. Four Yanks surrendered. Others ran away disappearing into the darkness.

"Follow me. Make for the Richmond and York River Railroad." Jesse turned Sam.

"There's Fusball Station. It's pretty close to Hanover and is on the Pamonkey. Look yonder at that Yankee wagon train. Those transports are surely loaded with stores. BURN 'EM. BURN 'EM."

Yank guns opened fire. In unison Rebel horsemen yelled. Three transports erupted in flames. Wagon after wagon caught fire. Yanks abandoned them and scurried to unite themselves.

Jesse's boys captured many wagons. The depot disappeared into flames and ashes. "Ride for the Chickahominy as fast as possible. Stay together. We're to ford it tomorrow."

SATURDAY/14. Jesse and William rode together. William said, "Look how the creek is rising. I've been noticing a bunch of heavy clouds north of us most every day lately."

In the night Jesse told his boys, "We're on the river's edge but it's too dark to see clearly. William's right about the rains. The river is in flood stage. We'll swim our horses across. Just flow with the current and wait for the horse behind you. Let's go." Sam splashed into the water.

"That was fun." William galloped his bay along the water's edge. Let's do it again."

"Come back here, you lame brain." Jesse opened his canteen and drank. "Our artillery is behind us; so find a narrow spot where we can build a bridge for them to cross."

Jesse watched the last cannon rumble across the bridge. "Thank heavens. Our timing was perfect. Here come the Yanks in full force. Cut the bridge loose."

"Ye hi. Look how those whirlpools tore that thing apart." A private grinned.

"The Chickahominy Swamp is going to be a nightmare for General McClellan's Army." Jesse packed tobacco into his corncob pipe. "Our artillery left a mire of ruts and loblollies. From our position we can kill every Yank who dares crossing the river."

General Jeb Stuart, commander of Lee's Cavalry, talked to the boys, "General Jackson's success in the Shenandoah Valley opened a way for Lee to take the offensive at Richmond. Our cavalry must ride completely around McClellan's Army."

Jesse led his column to Cole Wilcox. "Boys. It's about night. We haven't fed for better'n a day and a half. There's some grain on the wagons. Take care of your horses and rest a little."

An hour passed. Major Martin ordered, "Mount up. It's nine o'clock and twenty-five miles to Richmond. We'll push forward bringing these seventy-five prisoners along with 255 mules and horses."

SUNDAY/15. Jesse's column cheered when the Provost Marshal took charge of the prisoners and animals.

After the cavalrymen completely rode around McClellan's Army, General Stuart studied the findings sketched on the maps. He said,

"This confirms that McClellan's right flank is isolated by the rain-swollen Chickahominy."

General Lee said, "It was worth the gamble. We will move the mass of our forces from McClellan's front, join with Stonewall, and destroy the Union Army by shattering its exposed wing and taking them in flank."

THURSDAY/19. Jesse told his boys, "We'll leave Richmond and ride for the South Anna River. Our job is to remain along the river and picket until 26, June."

At daylight, skirmishes began when Jeb Stuart's Cavalry and Stonewall Jackson's "Foot Cavalry" attacked the Yankees on the right and rear. Riding beside Jesse, William laughed. "Look yonder. The Yanks are settin' fire to their camps and leaving. They have fled. YA HOO."

"Yeah. We've got to ride through their camps in line of barrage. Lend me a couple of crackers."

At two o'clock the Yanks took a stand. Jesse shouted to his column. "Hold it. There's a Rebel division moving in with good earnest."

His eyes darted from place to place while a superior Yank force emerged. At five o'clock Rebel re-enforcements marched in columns. All Rebels bounded in with a blood-curdling yell and drove the Yankees before them.

SATURDAY/28. "They call this 'Cold Harbor' and I'd say that we have a decided victory." Jesse held a small sack of grain to Sam's mouth.

"Yeah." William ate a cracker and piece of bacon. "Quartermaster passed word that General Lee's Army of Northern Virginia launched heavy assaults at Mechanicsville this morning. And General Fitz John Porter's Corps held."

"Thank goodness we've got a retreating Union Army here. Boy. I needed this little break.

Major Martin ordered, "Press forward. Kill every Yank in sight. Let's go. Let's go."

At daylight Jesse and William got off their horses and packed mixed feed into buckets. Quartermaster told them, "General Lee attacked Porter again. This time at Gaines' Mill. They had costly fighting but broke through the Federal lines. The Army of the Potomac is in full retreat towards the James River."

"All right. We've got to stay in pursuit." Jesse smiled.

SUNDAY/29. Major Martin relayed General Lee's orders. "Relentlessly, press forward. Destroy McClellan's Army."

Confederate forces attacked the Federals' rear.

MONDAY/30. At Frayser's Farm Rebels attacked General Randol's Battery. Just before dark Major Martin announced, "Something happened between our commanders' communications. General McClellan is a masterful trainer in executing skillful withdrawal tactics. We pressed them in full pursuit and they suckered us in. All of our attacks failed."

Jesse pointed to his right. "Look at that beautiful plantation home."

"I wonder if they'll share some food with us. If I had some grease I'd fry my belt." William tugged at his waist.

General Jeb Stuart commanded, "Take that house."

"Company C. Dismount. On foot. CHARGE." Major Martin crouched low in the sage.

Jesse scurried toward the northeast corner of the house. His column of men followed with weapons readied for firing. "Cover me. I'm going in."

An elderly lady screamed, "You nearly scared me to death, young man. What do you want?"

"I'm sorry, Mam. General Stuart wants to set up his headquarters on the first floor of your lovely home. It'll be just for a day or two."

"Well, all right. My husband rode into Richmond this morning. Our two sons are with Stonewall Jackson. We don't hear from them very often."

"I'm sure they don't have much time for writing." Jesse waved from the front porch and General Stuart hitched his horse. He tipped his hat to the lady.

"Jesse," William shouted from the kitchen. "Come 'ere. We found everything that's good to eat. Fresh cornbread. Ripe tomatoes. Roast. Baked potatoes. Buttermilk."

"You know better than to walk into a family's home and take their food." Jesse wiped his lips.

"All of you sit down to the table and I'll prepare the food for you. You act as if you're starving." The lady tied an apron around her.

General Stuart placed his hat on the floor beside his chair. "Mam, You are very kind to do this. And we thank you. Let's bow our heads."

"I'm in this war, too. The ladies of our church have gotten Confederate gray material and made summer-weight uniforms. We were going to send them to Richmond but if you boys can wear any of them you're welcome to them."

"Thank you, Mam." Jesse loaded uniforms onto Sam.

JULY, 1862

TUESDAY/1. "Mount-up, boys." Major Martin sat on his horse. "We're marching toward the Chickahominy."

WEDNESDAY/2. Jesse stopped Sam and watched a log float down stream. "We're back to the river."

"Here come the Yanks." An excited Rebel voice broke the silence.

Company C formed a barrage line and skirmished. The Yanks fell back. Jesse said, "Hold up. This is as far as we'll follow them."

Jesse led his column across the river. Late in the night he ordered, "Mount up and move out."

THURSDAY/3. Rain poured down. Company C rode under cover of a forest. Major Martin shouted. "Dismount. COMMENCE FIRING."

"These are pretty warm skirmishes." William smiled. "You better move away from that tree. A Yank has you in his sights."

Jesse crouched and looked up. "I heard one ball hit above my head but there are two lodged in the bark. He had them in a straight line. Thank goodness he aimed a little too high."

In unison Rebel Cavalry yelled and rushed the Yankees. Their lines broke. Rain poured. Yanks threw down their weapons and raised their hands. Jesse ordered, "Line 'em up and count heads."

"Two hundred and five." William wiped rain from his forehead.

FRIDAY/4. "The sun is just about straight up over head. Isn't this a wonderful way to celebrate Independence Day? These dew berries, bacon, and crackers beat no food at all." Jesse broke a cracker.

"Riding this picket and watching Yankee movements ain't bad duty. Wonder how our families are celebrating?" William stopped his horse and pointed.

"There are at least 2,000 Yanks moving up stream." Jesse got off Sam. "Stay low and out of sight."

SATURDAY/5. Company C met the 11th Regiment. A lieutenant told Jesse, "You know how secretive General Stonewall Jackson is. I heard that he rode fifty-three miles in just over twelve hours to meet with General Lee in Richmond."

"I heard he got there on 23, June."

"Generals Longstreet, A. P. Hill, and D. H. Hill met with them to plan destruction of General McClellan's Army of the Potomac.

"We need to beat them, because they are within five miles of Richmond." Jesse adjusted his saddle girth.

"I hear that most of the Union forces are south of the Chickahominy."

Jesse said, "We've been riding close to the river, and it is a swampy, steep-banked stream. On it northeast of Richmond, General Fitz John Porter's Corps took up a position north of the river, behind Beaver Dam Creek. General Stuart told General Lee that Porter's solitary corps was vulnerable."

The Lieutenant said, "If we could turn this flank and strike Porter's Corps and cut General McClellan's supply line, that'd force the Yanks to fight with a big disadvantage or retreat very quickly."

"Things didn't go as the generals planned. General Longstreet told General Jackson, 'You have distance to overcome, and in all probability the Yankees will be obstacles in the way of your march. As your move is the key to the campaign you should appoint the hour at which the connection may be made co-operative.'" Jesse leaned against Sam.

"Some of the generals said that Jackson failed five times during those Seven Days Battles. He isn't the same Stonewall as at Manassas." The lieutenant chewed a blade of grass.

"I don't know. He left the meeting and rode those long miles, separating his troops. He told General Longstreet that he'd meet them on 25, June. Reports say that his troops didn't march but one mile an hour on account of the rutty territory and this gosh-awful heat. By dark they were still five miles from their objective. He's bound to be worn out."

The Lieutenant said, "I heard, also, that the Yanks' gunboats provided heavy firepower and the James River a secure line of logistics."

Jesse smiled. "I imagine history books will teach that the Federal Artillery repulsed General Lee's Army at Malvern Hill, ending this Seven Days Campaign. I appreciate the information we've been able to share."

"I'm disappointed that General McClellan is safe but I'm glad his Peninsular Campaign is over."

Jesse mounted Sam. "I hope to see you again. Our company is going on picket for three days near Charles City Courthouse."

Other pickets sent word that General John Pope consolidated Union forces southwest of Washington and began marching southward along the Orange and Virginia Railroad.

WEDNESDAY/9. Jesse rode from Charles City Courthouse. He told William, "We're heading for camps five miles northwest of Richmond and on the James River."

"That's good. We can go fishing and capture some terrapins. Turtle soup is one of my favorites." William patted his stomach.

"You're always thinking about something to eat."

"Not really. I spend a lot of time thinking about girls. If a man has plenty to eat and a luscious girl in his arms he ought to be happy. I haven't held a girl since we left Hanover."

"We'll get food long before we get girls again."

"Yeah. But food's mighty scarce, too."

"Let me have your attention." Major Martin rode up hurriedly. "Part of General Pope's forces entered Culpeper yesterday and General Lee sent Generals Jackson and Ewell on trains to Gordonsville, a strategic railroad junction, until Army of Northern Virginia can move up and into position. Jackson has 10,000 men. I don't like the idea of moving on Sunday, the thirteenth, but we're ordered to Camp Discipline. That's close to Mechanicsville. For a week we'll drill at offense and defense types of warfare. Prepare to mount up."

MONDAY/21. Company C rode into camps at Charles City Courthouse. Jesse told William, "We need to learn as much as we can about the way successful generals operate."

"What do you mean?"

"Take General Stonewall Jackson for instance. His leadership style is with authority, secretive, and mighty unforgiving. Quartermaster heard that he put all his subordinate generals on court martial duty." Jesse plucked a blade of johnson grass and sucked juice from it.

"It's bitter hard to keep up with General Jackson. He gives orders swiftly but distinctly; then rides away. He tells his subordinates, 'Look there. See that railroad station? Take it.' And Boy, they better take it."

"That's what I mean. He knows what's got to happen and expects us make it happen."

THURSDAY/24. Jesse ordered, "Mount up. We're riding to Fredericksburg."

That night in Fredericksburg a scout reported, "The Yanks are about to cut us off with a large force."

FRIDAY/25. "All right." Major Martin studied a map. "It's almost 2:30 A.M. We'll put out for camps."

Company C reached North Anna River. "We'll stop here and picket. Jesse, take your column north and west."

"Yes, Sir."

SATURDAY/26. A scout reported a large force of Yankees moving toward camps. With twenty men Jesse rode out to meet them.

After an hour's ride he stopped and announced, "We've got a false report. Ride back to camps."

"Jesse, I've got to tell you something." William frowned.

"Okay?"

"You remember when I dragged that Yankee back there at the James River, near Williamsburg?"

"Yeah."

"I didn't say anything about it but something busted loose in my guts. I've been passing blood."

"You're going to sick call in the morning. I know you've been losing weight."

THURSDAY/31. Major Martin announced, "Prepare to move out. We're starting for camps at Hanover Courthouse."

AUGUST, 1862

FRIDAY/1. Company C fell in for drill. William frowned as he forced his leg over the saddle. Jesse said, "What did the doctor tell you?"

"Not much. Quartermaster said that on 29, July, General Banks' two divisions marched to support General Crawford at Cedar Run, eight miles south of Culpeper."

"Are you still bleeding?"

"Some. And General A. P. Hill's division brought General Jackson's force up to 28,000. They're at Gordonsville."

Major Martin said, "General Pope marched to the hamlet of Orange and General Jackson pressed on toward Culpeper."

FRIDAY/8. Early in the morning William walked from sick call slowly. "The doctor gave discharge papers to me. I'll leave y'all on the twelfth."

"Maybe you'll get well while you're home and come back in the cavalry. I'll write a letter to Sallie and you can deliver it to her personally. The Jeff Davis Legion rides for White Oak Swamps today. More picket."

"It's all over for me. Good luck. You'll always be my best friend." William turned away.

"I wish that I could go with you."

Jesse walked over to the supply wagons and filled his saddle bags with ammunition.

WEDNESDAY/13. Jesse and Major Martin rode with the Jeff Davis Legion into White Oak Swamps. Jesse said, "William Daniel and I understood each other. I reckon I'll look over our men and choose another partner."

"Sounds good. In the meantime we'll cover each other." Major Martin walked towards Headquarters.

"How're you and Major Martin getting' along?" Quartermaster smiled.

"Great. Why?" Jesse looked puzzled.

"I don't know. He told me that he was glad William left. You know that General John Pope has organized what the Yanks call, 'The Army of Virginia?'"

"Yeah."

"Well, they marched to the hamlet of Orange on 7, August. Union Generals Crawford and Banks secured Culpeper. They didn't know that General Jackson was bringing his army of 28,000 north from Gordonsville. His division leaders are Generals A. P. Hill, Winder, and Ewell."

"If what you're telling me is correct, I think we'll hear about a big fight. In fact, they might send us to help General Lee. What happened at Cedar Mountain?"

"General Jackson's foot cavalry normally moves rapidly. He complained about General Hill's slowness. All three divisions moved slowly, having 93 supply wagons. Jackson planned to arrive at Culpeper on 8, August. He didn't know that Yankee troops were already there.

"You asked about Cedar Mountain. It lies six miles south of Culpeper along Cedar Run. It was here that the Union and Confederate Armies clashed.

"One of our cavalrymen told Jackson, 'Up ahead is an unknown number of Yankee troops and they're supported with cannon.'

"Jackson dispatched our artillery. They posted cannons along the main road on the shoulder of Cedar Mountain and to their left on a small knoll.

For three hours our artillery fought theirs. A Yank projectile killed General Winder."

"Aw. No." Jesse frowned.

"General Jackson rode with his aides along the narrow road choked with men, horses, and artillery. Before he reached the forward units the Yanks hit with a surprise flank attack. Under cover of the artillery duel Union troops advanced through thick woods on our left and broke through the thin infantry defense.

"Fugitives threw down their weapons and ran away from the overwhelming hail of lead. Jackson met them. He drew his sword. The men stopped. Jackson turned to a courier and shouted, 'Tell Hill to bring his men up at once.'

"Hill's division came forward, the fugitives regrouped, and a counterattack drove back the exhausted Union troops. They left their wounded and dead in the woods. Hill's troops pushed forward. Far to their right, General Ewell's division advanced with Hill's. Darkness settled over Cedar Mountain.

"Another hot day dawned on Sunday, 10, August. A Union party bearing a flag of truce requested permission to treat their wounded and bury their dead.

"General Jackson withdrew his men under cover of a dark summer night and crossed the Rapidan and Robinson rivers. Yanks didn't pursue."

FRIDAY/22. Riding into camp from picketing, Jesse watched the sun creep over the trees. He fed a bucket of mixed feed to Sam and walked to the cooks. One of them handed a bacon biscuit to him. Jesse said, "Where is General Lee?"

"Don't know."

"I've been riding all night, I'm hungry, and Major Martin orders a ride to Hanover."

"That's life."

SATURDAY/23. Dead-tired, Jesse stretched out on the ground in Hanover. He nestled his head on a large oak root and snored within seconds.

SUNDAY/24, Major Martin ordered, "Company C, MOUNT UP. Listen now. We'll ride toward Huderson Station. We'll depart there on 26, August, and arrive Warrenton on 30, August. Any questions?"

During the Rebel cavalry's movements General Stonewall Jackson destroyed the Yank's main supply base at Manassas. His men pillaged the depot, loaded their wagons with usable rifles, ammunition and food; then made ready to leave.

Jackson's forces moved to a position in the woods to Groveton near the Manassas battlefield.

General Lee said to his staff, "I want to destroy Pope before McClellan's Army joins him. We'll divide our forces by sending Stonewall on a sweep northward through Thoroughfare Gap, and around Pope's Army."

Union General Pope, stung by the attack on his supply base, abandoned the line of the Rappahannock and headed toward Manassas to "bag" Jackson. At the same time, to unify his army, Lee moved northward with General Longstreet's Corps.

On the afternoon of 28, August, Jackson ordered his troops to attack on a Union column that marched by on the Warrenton Turnpike. He said, "This should prevent Pope's efforts to concentrate at Centreville and bring him to battle."

At Brawner's Farm a savage battle raged until dark.

General Pope told his staff, "I'm convinced that Jackson is isolated. Converge our columns on Groveton. I'm sure we can destroy Jackson before Lee and Longstreet intervene."

On 29, August, Pope's Army found Jackson's troops posted along an unfinished railroad grade north of the Warrenton Turnpike. Pope hurled his men against Jackson's. All afternoon there erupted a series of uncoordinated attacks. Momentarily the Yanks broke through Jackson's lines in several places. Each time Rebels forced Yanks back.

Pope failed to learn that General Longstreet's troops arrived on the battlefield during the afternoon and deployed on Jackson's right, overlapping the Union's exposed left.

General Lee told Longstreet, "Attack."

"The time is just not right." Old Pete sent word back to Lee.

On 30, August, Lee marched the remainder of his Army onto the battlefield. The morning passed quietly.

Pope ordered, "The Confederates are retreating. Pursue them."

Within thirty minutes a messenger came to General Pope. "General Lee hasn't gone anywhere."

"Attack Jackson's line." Pope shouted.

Union General Fitz John Porter's Corps and some of McDowell's Corps struck Confederate General Stark's Division at "Deep Cut," an unfinished section of railroad. Rebels held firm. Their aim was precise. Yankee soldiers collapsed on the battlefield. Blood soaked through uniforms and oozed into the ground. Porter's column hurled back.

Confederate General Longstreet watched the confused Union lines. "Our columns are massive compared to theirs. Move forward and stagger their left flank."

"Our army is faced with annihilation." General Pope looked into frantic eyes of his staff. "Regroup on Chinn Ridge."

Rebels pressed on.

"Follow me to Henry Hill House and take a stand. General Pope drew his sword.

"All right. It's nearly dark, and we've bought time on Chinn Ridge and Henry Hill. We'll withdraw, cross Bull Run, and move toward our Washington defenses. Lee's bold and brilliant strategy has cost us Manassas a second time." Pope rode northward to the Warrenton Turnpike.

SEPTEMBER, 1862

MONDAY/1. Jesse rode from Warrenton and crossed Manassas Battlefield. He and Major Martin pointed to dead soldiers. Jesse said, "In every direction I look I see men lying sprawled on bloody ground. What an awesome sight."

"Yeah." Major adjusted his hat to shade his eyes. "I stopped on the Stone Bridge where I heard General Lee say that an estimated 23,936 men lay dead here. Washington reported 14,462 Yankees killed and we lost 9,474. And that's just one day."

"What did General Lee say about our invading the North?"

"Excuse me." Major vomited. "He said that this victory ought to open our way for our first invasion of northern territory. And some real good news is that we have a bid for foreign intervention.

"General Lee tried to divide Pope's retreating army at Chantilly but failed. During the assault a Rebel shot and killed General Phillip Kearney. He won't be riding his beautiful jet-black horse anymore."

"Great."

TUESDAY/2. Company C rode into Fairfax Courthouse, skirmished, and drove the Yanks out.

"Pursue them," Jesse shouted. His eyes squinted after the sun dropped below the horizon. He scrubbed his knee against a large tree.

Suddenly Yanks screamed and charged from the trees alongside the main road. Jesse swung his sword at a blurred figure.

"Watch out. You nearly hit me." Major Martin stopped his horse.

"Assemble. Follow me." Jesse turned Sam and rode back to the edge of town.

"Count off."

Each man shouted his number.

"All right. They didn't damage us much. The night is too dark to distinguish them from us. We'll bed down here out of sight." Jesse walked Sam into a thicket. Mud squished under foot.

"You know, Jesse." Major Martin loosened his horse's girth. "General Lee wants to invade the North for several reasons."

"What are they? Other than he wants to destroy Washington." Jesse sipped water from his canteen.

Major said, "We're not ready for that yet. We've defeated Union forces time and time again throughout Virginia. They're bound to be demoralized. General Lee's emotions are touched about his beloved state of Virginia. Look around us. Giant destruction is all over."

"You think he wants to get out of Virginia?"

"Yeah. And here's Maryland. We need to add her to our cause and the odds look good right now. And I tell you General Lee wants recognition from Europe. It may lead to their sending aid to the Confederacy and that's essential to ultimate victory for us."

"Where do we go from here?" Jesse unfurled his blanket.

"Maryland."

WEDNESDAY/3. Jesse rode into Camps at Danksville and picketed there.

FRIDAY/5. "Mount up. Proceed to Leesburg." Major Martin sat erect in his saddle.

Company C mustered on the Potomac's west bank by 8:00 P. M. An hour later every horse and rider mustered on Maryland soil. They pressed on to Barville and camped for the night.

North and west of the cavalry General Lee's columns marched into Maryland occupying Frederick.

Major Martin told Jesse, "We just swept frustration all over General McClellan and his whole Army of the Potomac."

"Why do you say that?"

"Because Mac decided to follow General Lee. The Yanks didn't know what to do. They moved very cautiously and that cost them time. They're scared to death of General Stonewall Jackson and don't know where he is. Mac knows about our cavalry's brutal attacks. We don't plan to leave a man standing."

SATURDAY/6. Company C rode through Barville and Urbana, Maryland. They camped near Urbana.

WEDNESDAY/10. Jesse rode picket. When he returned to camp he told Major Martin, "If all of Maryland is the same as Urbana, Maryland is on our side. I must say in behalf of the citizens here, I never was treated better anywhere while on picket. A good lady sent dinner to me but I lost it because some Yanks came and I had to run."

"Company C, mount up. Proceed on this road to Frederick." Major Martin moved his right hand forward. Jesse guided Sam along the major's left.

They rode through Frederick's Main Street. A voice shouted, "YANKS TO OUR RIGHT."

During the skirmish that followed Jesse's sword pricked a Yankee Colonel's throat. "Surrender or I'll slit you from ear to ear."

"I surrender." His voice quivered.

Jesse's column surrounded several Yank prisoners and moved them to the wagons.

FRIDAY/12. Jesse rode through Fairen. Company C set up camp for the night at the town's edge. From the hill's highest point Jesse looked north, east, south, and west.

"Jesse, you and your column ride picket tonight." Major Martin drank water from his canteen and belched. "Excuse me."

"Yes, Sir." His voice rasped.

That night, he and his men observed every direction of surrounding territory. A voice broke the silence. "Over there to the west. See those rockets?"

"Yeah. Keep count of them." Jesse looked. "I've counted twenty-five sky rockets and some of them are coming from Sugarloaf Mountain."

SATURDAY/13. A cool breeze touched Jesse's face while he rode into camp. He reported to Major Martin, "Sir, this is a beautiful morning and I hate to tell you that we can expect the Yanks at every moment."

"Aw, Jesse." Major Martin smiled. "This good gentleman is broiling some chickens for us. Drink a little of his imported whiskey and you can handle those Yanks."

When the sun was an hour high the Yanks came into sight and charged. Jesse, with two other men, braced against a large oak. Jesse said, "Wait until you see the whites of their eyes; then fire."

Three shots rang out. A horse fell dead. The Yanks continued coming. Jesse said, "I find it convenient to give them the road. Let's skedaddle and join the company for an ambush."

Company C charged and the Yanks retreated.

An hour later the Yanks came up in strong force. For six hours Company C fought them. A minnie ball smashed into John Robinson's left arm. He screamed.

On the left Rebels yelled and killed many Yanks. Pursued closely Company C moved out when the sun shone down from straight overhead. They rode into Middletown. Here they checked the Yanks; however, suffered some while passing through. Two miles from this place they met their infantry. Jesse told John Robinson, "All is right."

They rode through Boonsboro, Maryland. John said, "You're wrong. While the doctor took the minnie out of my arm the medics talked about a lost order of General Lee's. They called it Special Orders #191. While General Hampton had us riding west out of Frederick, the Indiana 27th marched in from the east. They found our campground and stayed there."

"We left a mess for them." Jesse smiled.

"There was more than a mess. Listen to this. Yankee Corporal Martin Mitchell and First Sergeant John Blass were stretched out on the ground resting. The corporal's curiosity got the best of him while they talked about a long bulky envelope, lying in the grass. He found a long paper full of writing and wrapped around three cigars.

"The envelope was addressed to Major General D. H. Hill, Commanding Division. The orders were filled with names of General Jackson, Longstreet, and McLaws. Sergeant ran those lost orders #191 to their captain; he to regimental headquarters; then to Sumner Corp's brigade commands; he to Brigadier General A. S. Williams. Colonel Pittman stuffed the orders into his pocket and ran his horse all the way to General McClellan's Headquarters."

"Maybe those orders will scare the pants off General McClellan and he'll be over cautious as usual." Jesse sharpened his knife.

"Let's hope so. General Lee sent General Jackson with 25,000 to take Harper's Ferry."

Jesse said, "That should secure our gateway to the Shenandoah Valley."

"The remainder of the Army of Northern Virginia is marching toward Hagerstown, Maryland."

SUNDAY/14. Company C rode through Cedarsville. They fought very hard all day in the South Mountains. They began on the Potomac River across from Harper's Ferry, ran deep into Pennsylvania, and passed a few miles west of Gettysburg. They were a large, slowly curving ridge.

"Jesse." Major Martin adjusted a stick of firewood. "You want a cup of coffee?"

"Does a horse eat mixed feed?" He reached into his saddlebag and his rag doll fell to the ground. Jesse looked at Major and smiled.

"Don't expect me to talk about Madge. I know about your knocking out the quartermaster." Major poured a cup of coffee.

"Where are General McClellan's forces?" Jesse sipped.

"When McClellan looks at his western horizon today he sees this long bluish-green curtain and he knows that behind this curtain lay the striking power of the Confederacy, more particularly the Army of Northern Virginia, hidden securely. We fought those Yanks today because they were trying to find our infantry. Every road the Yankee cavalry took led into General Stuart's patrols. General Lee has all the advantage."

MONDAY/15. Near midnight Jesse's patrol rode as an advance guard for their wagon train. They crossed the Potomac at Williamsport, Maryland, passed through Shepherdstown, and re-crossed the Potomac.

Riding across the bridge Jesse told Major Martin, "I watched you look over those girls along the streets. There were more pretty ladies in Shepherdstown than any other place I've ever been."

"You've been away from Mississippi too long."

TUESDAY/16. At nightfall Company C drew up into a line and dismounted. Most of the men lay down and some were already asleep when their horses took a scare. All except six got away. They ran through the company's pickets and into a Yankee line. The Yankees shot. Horses turned back. Many hurt themselves and numbers were lost.

Major Martin returned from a staff meeting. "While we were moving yesterday General Stonewall Jackson captured Harper's Ferry. General A. P. Hill's Division was with him. They moved in from the south. General McLaws fought his way up the steep ridge of Maryland Heights on the north side of the Potomac and General John Walker marched his men to Loudown Heights and attacked from the east.

"But General McClellan fought his way through South Mountain passes."

"General Lee studied his predicament at Sharpsburg, Maryland. The Potomac was at his back. His army was inferior numerically because of Jackson's absence; so most of Jackson's forces will rejoin Lee today."

WEDNESDAY/17. All hell broke loose at daylight. Jesse fought at Sharpsburg until darkness fell. He was five miles from the Potomac. He and some of his men rode to the wagon train and loaded ammunition. Quartermaster told them, "General McClellan launched powerful but unjointed attacks which probably will make Antietam Creek the bloodiest single day of the war, thus far.

"General Lee repulsed those assaults due to skillful and timely arrival of General A. P. Hill's Light Division. His men double-timed across seventeen miles from Harper's Ferry and delivered a surprise flank attack on the Yanks' left. I heard that over 25,000 men fell dead or wounded during the day."

TUEDAY/18. "Reveille. Reveille." Sergeant scurried through camp. "Both armies are sending out flags of truce long enough to bury the dead."

Company C's men dug trenches, threw dead bodies into them, and covered their remains with dirt. At midnight Company C crossed the river.

FRIDAY/19. Riding on toward Williamsport Jesse said to John Robinson, "I expect we'll bag some Yankees any minute now."

"I'm ready." John placed the musket in his right hand.

No Yanks confronted them. The company rode into Williamsport and camped there.

SUNDAY/28. They re-crossed the Potomac, rode on to Aimesville and set-up camp. Major Martin announced to the company, "Boys, General Lee's high hopes for beating the Yankees ended at Sharpsburg; so, in a way we got beat at Antietam Creek."

Jesse said, "In another way though, we beat the Yankees. If General McClellan had held out General Lee couldn't have moved his army back into Virginia."

"You're right." Major Martin continued. "Five days after our intense fighting President Lincoln issued a draft of what he calls the Emancipation

Proclamation. This bold decree grants freedom to all slaves remaining in seceded states. His effective date will be 1, January, 1863."

"There's no way for President Lincoln to preserve the Union now." John Robinson sipped from his canteen.

"This decree might hinder involvement by European countries to help the confederacy." Jesse dropped his saddle to the ground.

TUESDAY/30. Major Martin read their orders, "Ride to Winchester, Virginia."

"MOUNT UP." Jesse Shouted.

They rode through Starksville and entered Martinsburg. Major Martin stopped his horse and said, "Boys, they must have named this city after my folks. I understand some stragglers are here. Break up into columns, search up and down, back and forth; then report back here in two hours."

Jesse and John Robinson rode beside each other. After a while Jesse said, "This is a beautiful large place. Let's check the tavern."

They hitched their horses and walked in. Four Rebel soldiers scampered from a table, overturning bottles.

"Halt or I'll kill you." Jesse leveled his pistol at them.

The soldiers stopped and raised their hands

"John, take these boys back to Major Martin while I search for more." Jesse walked from the tavern and led Sam toward a corner.

After two hours Major Martin counted thirty-one deserters. "We'll spend tonight on the outskirts and begin October by riding over to Little North Mountain. Turn over these deserters to their commands and set up camp."

OCTOBER, 1862

SATURDAY/18. They moved camp one mile, at which site they remained.

THURSDAY/23. Major Martin ordered, "Mount up and move camp to Martinsburg."

FRIDAY/24. In late morning they set up camp near Martinsburg.

WEDNESDAY/29. While scouting Jesse rode out nine miles northwest of Martinsburg. At noon near Hedgeville, a private yelled, "Yank pickets straight ahead."

The Yanks fired a volley. Cherry and Scarbrough's horses fell, blood dribbled from their sides. Jesse's eyes scanned his men. Four scampered on foot from the Yankees. Jesse watched John Daniel and laughed. "Run, John. Jump."

An old black mare stood unbridled in the field. Swiftly John jumped, placed his hands on her hips, and plopped straddle her back. He kicked and yelled, leaned and snatched her mane. The old mare ran the home stretch as fast as any.

"Boy, that was close. I think I'll keep her." John laughed. "Find a bridle for me."

Back in camp Jesse listened to Major Martin. "We missed some excitement with General Stuart."

"What do you mean?" Jesse drank some coffee.

"On 10, October, General Stuart, with that plume in his hat led 1800 cavalrymen towards Chambersburg, Pennsylvania. They left from Darkesville west of Harper's Ferry and rode across the Potomac into Maryland. Thence through Mercersburg, Pennsylvania, reaching Chambersburg by dark. They destroyed machine shops and Yankee supply warehouses on the Cumberland Valley Railroad. They left on 11, October, and came back through Maryland, by way of Emmitsburg, Hyattstown, and Barnesville. They crossed the Potomac at Leesburg, Virginia, early on 12, October. They covered a total of 126 miles, riding the last 80 non-stop in less than 36 hours."

"General Stuart is unbelievable. He makes my spirits soar sky high. I'd ride to hell and back with him." Jesse's eyes sparkled. "This makes the second time he's ridden around McClellan's Army of the Potomac. I'm sure the cavalry gathered valuable information for General Lee."

NOVEMBER, 1862

MONDAY/3. Company C rode away from Martinsburg, Maryland. At the edge of town Major Martin stopped his horse. "Give me your attention.

"We've been ordered to re-enforce General Stuart at Barber's Cross Roads."

TUESDAY/4. They passed through Millwood, White Post, and through the Blue Ridge Mountain at Manassas Gap.

WEDNESDAY/5. The enemy came up very early at Barber's Cross Roads. Rebel artillery opened fire. Jesse and Major Martin watched. Jesse said, "Thank goodness for our artillery. They surely checked those Yanks. Now, if they can hold until 3:00 P.M., the First North Carolina Regiment will join us."

"You must be in touch with our Maker." Major Martin held his watch. "It's 2:50 and there are the Carolinas. They saved our cavalry skirmishers. Look at those Yanks fall. Let's move out."

The company rode to Flint Hill and camped.

THURSDAY/6. Jesse and his men watched alertly for Yanks. When the sun inched toward the western horizon Yanks marched into range. Jesse yelled, "CHARGE."

Yanks held for fifteen minutes; then ran back.

Company C rode to Little Washington. Major Martin rode up to headquarters while the men set up camp. Upon returning Major announced, "Boys, we'll be here until 8, November. We can drill and relax a little."

FRIDAY/7. Quartermaster told Jesse, "President Lincoln's patience ran out with General McClellan because he didn't show enough initiative. A Washington newspaper wrote that General Ambrose Burnside is taking over the Union Army."

"Word leaked out from a Washington advisor who approved Mr. Lincoln's decision." Jesse whittled some chips into a pile. He looked off into the distance. "General Burnside proposed that the Union Army move secretly and swiftly to Fredericksburg, cross the Rappahannock River on pontoon bridges, and advance straight on to Richmond."

"Looks to me like we're headin' towards Fredericksburg." Quartermaster stuffed tobacco into a corncob pipe.

"I reckon we'll be ridin' picket in this area." Jesse closed his knife and walked toward his tent.

SATURDAY/8. A line formed for breakfast. Jesse asked, "Who robbed a henhouse?"

"Don't ask any questions." The cook smiled. "Just to show how much we like you, how do you want your eggs cooked?"

"Fry mine hard on both sides."

"The reason Cookie likes you so much this morning is because you're riding toward Staunton. This is 8, November, isn't it?" Major Martin sipped coffee from a tin cup.

"Staunton? This is the 8th all right. But why am I going to Staunton?" Jesse cut into an egg with his fork.

"We've got a shipment of new uniforms down there and you're going down to supervise their safe delivery."

"That's worth a ride to Staunton." Jesse shook pepper over his eggs.

"Look. The boys are so proud that you're going they saddled-up Sam for you. Ride, Boy."

Jesse spent that night at a Mrs. Hudson's.

SUNDAY/9. Early he mounted Sam, rode to the Rapidan, and boarded a railroad car. The train puffed into the Staunton Depot at dark. Jesse rode Sam to the warehouse.

Several shipping clerks gathered around a table on which Jesse emptied items he had collected from dead Union soldiers. "What will someone offer me for this pearl handled knife. It's brand new. Made in Europe."

"I'll give you this coon-skin cap and genuine bone handled knife. Winter's comin', you know."

"It's a deal." Jesse smiled. "What about this gold cross and chain. It'll be mighty pretty around your sweetheart's neck."

"I'll give you fifty dollars."

"Sold."

TUESDAY/11. In the early morning the chief warehouse clerk told Jesse, "Your company set up camp southwest of Madison Courthouse. We'll load your stores on a baggage car and you can be on your way."

"I'll be as welcome as the flowers in May. Our uniforms are just about worn to frazzles."

WEDNESDAY/12. Jesse found their camps.

THURSDAY/13. Major Martin read his orders, "Proceed to Culpeper and follow the railroad toward Brandy Station."

WEDNESDAY/19. Major Martin gave a report, "General Burnside's plans didn't unfold as well as he wrote them. When the Union vanguard reached Fredericksburg on 17, November, there wasn't a pontoon bridge in sight. His army couldn't cross the Rappahannock River.

"By the time pontoons arrived General Lee's army was fully entrenched on the heights immediately south of Fredericksburg.

"We're ridin' toward Woodville. That's almost due northwest from here. Mount up."

SUNDAY/23. They rode to Camp Modin which is twelve miles from Culpeper. Jesse rode picket along the Rappahannock River.

TUESDAY/25. He returned to camp.

THURSDAY/27. Major Martin ordered, "Company C will ride a scout on the Rappahannock. There's got to be some Yankees. Find and destroy them. Any questions?"

Late that night after the company bedded down, a sentry awakened Jesse. "I can see Yank campfires about a quarter mile down stream."

"Thanks. If they make any move let me know. Awaken me at five o'clock." Jesse tightened the blanket around his neck.

FRIDAY/28. Before daylight Company C loaded their weapons and led their horses down stream. In the dusk they formed around the Yanks. Jesse mounted Sam. His men mounted. He shouted, "CHARGE."

Rebel yells penetrated morning silence. Muskets crackled. Half dressed Yanks scurried about. A few jumped into the muddy river. John Robinson grinned. "I ain't no good sportsman. I shoot river-swimmin' deer."

Fire leaped from his musket. A red blotch drifted with the river's current.

Ninety Yankee cavalrymen held their arms heavenward. Jesse ordered, "Line up single file. Keep those hands up high and follow that rider. You won't get hurt. We'll take over your horses and all this fine equipment."

Jesse turned to John Robinson. "Ride back to Camp Modin and tell Major Martin to send some help out here to pick up these horses and wagons."

DECEMBER, 1862

MONDAY/1. Company C rode picket along the Rappahannock. No Yanks.

SATURDAY/6. Major W. E. Martin shouted, "Company C, Attention. As of today our command is under Colonel W. T. Martin."

"Thank you William. As far as I know, we are no kin. I'm proud of your company's record. Today we will ride out of Camp Modin and scout toward Centreville. Return on the 8th."

Riding beside, John Jesse said, "This freezing wind feels as if it's cutting me in two."

"If it calms down I think we'll be ridin' in snow. Look at those low dark clouds to our west. The pain in my arm is acting up. I'm sure it's from the changing weather." John buttoned up.

"You've hardly gotten the words out of your mouth and look at this snow. But the wind keeps on blowing." Jesse wiped his nose on his glove.

MONDAY/8. In three to four inches of snow Company C returned to Camp Modin. Quartermaster issued each man four day's rations.

The company assembled. Colonel Martin told them, "We've got an hour. Feed your horses and check your foul weather gear. We're riding a scout toward Dumfries. Dismissed."

TUESDAY/9. In early morning they ran into and skirmished some Yankees, capturing forty-nine plus some wagons.

Jesse told Colonel Martin, "These wagons are loaded with sutler's stores. Some of our boys are hurting. Is it all right with you if we stock up our saddle bags with fresh gear?"

"All is fair in love and war and we ain't fightin' for love."

Jesse found a good pair of boots. "I'll just trade mine for these. And these new boot socks don't have holes in their heels. Heaven doesn't feel any better than this. And I'll take some new gauntlets. I'll throw away these old rags I've been using for handkerchiefs."

SATURDAY/13. Company C rode into camp. They turned over to the provost their prisoners and thirteen wagons.

Colonel Martin advised his staff, "General Lee assembled his army at Fredericksburg. His watch-dogs, the cavalry, looked and waited for the Union's new general of the Army of the Potomac, General Burnside, to begin crossing the Rappahannock. Dense fog reduced visibility to nearly zero in cold, predawn darkness. It shrouded Fredericksburg.

"Brigadier General William Barksdale's Mississippi pickets shivvered in the raw morning air, standing guard along the river's banks. They guarded the eastern edge of town.

"The Army of the Potomac crossed the Rappahannock on 11, December. Two sharp booms from Confederate cannons broke the silence, signaling General Longstreet's Corps that the Union Army was making a move.

"This morning General Burnside hurled his divisions in piecemeal frontal assaults against General Lee's position. Our Confederate artillery and infantry ripped apart wave after wave of blue-coated troops. Now, that we've ridden almost every inch of the grounds near the river can't you imagine those Yanks trying to climb those bluffs and our guns tearing them to pieces?

"We'll remain in camps at Dumfries for a few days and wait for further orders."

FRIDAY/19. Colonel Martin ordered, "Company C, Mount up. There's a Yankee picket line three miles north of Dumfries. Let's go."

The cavalry Rebel-yelled, attacked the picket, and captured many. Jesse said, "I saw three get away."

"Ride hard, north and west toward Occoquan."

Colonel Martin spurred his horse.

Near the town John Robinson pointed. "There's a mess of Yankees and wagons."

"Run Circles around them. Rapid fire. Don't let them see you. When I go in you go in." Colonel Martin waved his hat.

Many Yanks threw down their weapons. Company C moved in and took them for prisoners.

Suddenly the enemy in full force came from nowhere. Rebel cavalry abandoned those wagons having mule teams. Jesse watched from a short distance. He had stopped at a tree stump and was cutting a piece of cheese. He dropped the cheese onto the stump, rode Sam into the skirmish, and fired several rounds.

He and John rode back to the stump, "Well, I offered some cheese to you but someone ate it."

"Thieving Yankees."

Rebels rode into camp while 135 prisoners walked. 170 horses pranced nervously, some hitched to 30 wagons loaded with a fine lot of sutler's stores.

MONDAY/22. Company C moved camp to ground within three miles of Culpeper Courthouse.

THURSDAY/25. Christmas Day began with an elegant breakfast stolen from Yankees. While the day passed several boys drank spirits and became quite lively.

That night Jesse rode out of camp going on a scout.

SATURDAY/27. General Wade Hampton ordered Company C, along with the whole brigade, to make their way back to camp at Dumfries. Nine miles from said place, at two A.M., they met two divisions led by Generals Fitzhugh Lee and W. H. F. "Rooney" Lee. General Jeb Stuart commanded these three brigades.

Quartermaster told Jesse, "The two Lees' brigades attacked the Yanks at Dumfries. They found a large force and had a draw-off, loosing only one man."

"I'm glad we scouted near Culpeper."

SUNDAY/28. Jesse's men rested until daylight. They mounted up and rode toward Occoquan. They met and charged approximately two hundred Yankee cavalry who broke into a run. Jesse shouted, "Spur up."

Soon they caught a great many. Others continued for six miles. Along the way Stuart's cavalry killed thirty Yanks.

General Stuart's whole command pushed forward and soon safely crossed the Occoquan River. They rode to Burk's Station where they secured a large quantity of tents, cooking equipment, medical supplies, and ammunition.

WEDNESDAY/31. Jesse sipped from a cup of hot coffee. "John, as I look back over the year of 1862, I see Yankee forces assailing Virginia from almost every approach. They marched to a line within nine miles of Richmond."

"Yeah, but tonight the only Federals within fifty miles of the city are prisoners of war or those frustrated from suffering defeat." John tugged at a boot.

JANUARY, 1863

THURSDAY/1. Company C moved forward toward camps near James City. Riding leisurely Jesse heard a scout yell, "Blue Coats marching straight for us."

"Charge." Jesse spurred Sam. Muskets crackled. Rebel-yells filled the air. Horses crunched into foot soldiers who wore blue uniforms. Company C captured more than 300 prisoners.

Jesse looked over the skirmish area. Many Rebels' horses lay dead and dying. He listened to horses and men, moaning.

At dark Company C settled down in camp.

WEDNESDAY/7. Colonel W. T. Martin stood before Company C. "Boys, I didn't get to stay with you very long. I want you to know that I think you're among the best of Confederate Cavalry. I'm leaving you today for a new command in Mississippi. Good luck and God-speed."

Jesse emptied a bucket of mixed feed into a box. Sam gulped it down. Fresh sacks of corn filled the warehouse. Hay reached the rafters on a barn. "John, isn't this a great blessing? Look at the abundance of hay and corn for our horses."

"Colonel Martin granted permission for you and me to ride into town tonight. The folks there have parties for soldiers regularly. I want to saddle-soap and oil my bridle and saddle." John held a water bucket.

"Sam is filthy from dust and dried blood. I'll warm a bucket of water and bathe him. Our horses ought to shine when we ride to a party." Jesse smiled.

They rode to Main Street wide and muddy. A lantern lighted a sign, "Town Hall." A long line of horses stood hitched outside. John held the front door while Jesse walked through.

"Welcome to James City." An old stooped man warmed his back near a red-hot, pot-bellied stove. "The fiddlers are just tuning up for a dance. Y'all must be members of the cavalry."

"We ride a horse now and then." Jesse shook hands with the old man and smiled.

"Enjoy y'all selves finely. We have good music, pretty girls, and smooth bottled spirits. You don't live but once you know."

THURSDAY/8. Almost every day now, little boys crowded into camp during afternoons. They ran from soldier to soldier, shouting, "Get your hot apple pie here. Only fifty cents. Get your pie. Fifty cents."

Jesse handed a dollar to a little boy. "What do you hear about peace?"

"Teacher said that it might come any time now. Y'all whip the Union Army every time you fight them. You want two, Mister?"

"Yeah, thanks. I hope you're right."

SATURDAY/17. Captain Henry arrived in camp. He announced, "Boys, we'll remain in camps near James City until 25, January; then ride toward Wolftown."

MONDAY/26. Company C rode into Wolftown.

TUESDAY/27. Jesse rode out of camp early, starting on picket.

WEDNESDAY/28. Snow fell all day, accumulating to ten inches. Jesse remained on picket.

SATURDAY/31. He rode back into camp. Some snow melted but more fell a few days later and measured fifteen inches. Forage for the cavalry's horses arrived on wagons.

Jesse and John walked across a drill field, and located Company H. Captain Hudson introduced himself to them. Jesse said, "Sir, Company C challenges Company H to a snowball battle commencing at 9:00 A.M."

"Company C has just announced its death warrant. Give us thirty minutes to plan our attack. Is this battle on horseback?" Captain Hudson grinned.

"On foot, Sir. Whenever a man gets hit in vital parts of his body he is to fall into the snow and becomes a casualty. He reports to the other's camp and is out of the game. We'll fight you to the last man."

Officers marched in their leadership positions. Enlisted men formed into lines of battle. Flag bearers held their colors high. Drummer boys beat their drums.

Many men packed snow into balls and stored them in metal buckets. The skinniest formed front lines and threw snowballs at their enemy.

For two hours the snowball battle raged. John Robinson was the last man standing for Company C. He dodged and ran from two men, counterattacked, but finally slipped and fell. The two men smashed snow all over his body.

Company C cooks prepared fresh coffee for Company H. They unloaded plenty of forage for horses and food for the men.

FEBRUARY, 1863

TUESDAY/24. Company C started a ride for Rockbridge County.

WEDNESDAY/25. They marched across the Blue Ridge Mountains, following a very crooked route. Stopping on the mountain top Jesse pointed. "I believe I can see twenty miles in front of us."

"Yeah, and did you look back?" You can see just as far in both directions."
John spurred his horse.

They rode through Mount Hope and camped one mile from said place.

THURSDAY/26. After riding a few hours they arrived at Honeyville. Jesse told his men, "Set-up camp and feed your horses. We've got wheat and hay for them."

During their stay at Honeyville they drilled.

MARCH, 1863

MONDAY/2. They marched to a suitable camp near Lamay.

FRIDAY/6. Company C rode north, following the Shenandoah River for twelve miles. Jesse said, "Boys, we'll camp here, but the only feed we have for our horses is a little wheat and hay."

SATURDAY/14. Horses' shoes knocked sparks from rocks in the road. Company C marched toward McGaheysville. They remained over night.

SUNDAY/15. They rode early to near Cross Keys, through Mount Sidney Station of Greenville, and on through Midway. Within a mile of said place they camped.

THURSDAY/19. Snow commenced falling. Wind mixed with snow. That night Jesse tightened his blanket around his neck. He flip-flopped on the ground. Finally he spoke to John, "Would the boys think we are a little peculiar if we slept back to back?"

"I really don't care what they think. I'd rather sleep back to back than be miserable."

Snow continued whispering outside.

FRIDAY/20. At daylight Jesse stretched. "Our tent feels warmer. Snow is fifteen inches deep on our tent pole."

"I hope the cooks can fix some breakfast. Thank goodness we've got plenty of corn and hay for our horses. This wind could nearly cut them in two." Jesse buttoned up his coat.

THURSDAY/26. They rode from Midway, heading for Rockbridge County. Riding through a small town, Brownsburg, Jesse pointed to several young girls. "Look over yonder."

"Oh Boy, you're missing a whole bunch of beauties. They're waving from the church steps. Wave, Jesse." John jumped off his horse, ploughed through snow drifts, hugged several girls, and they kissed his cold cheeks.

Company C rode through Cedar Grove, Jordan Springs, or Rockbridge. They found the North River one mile from here and set up camp.

SATURDAY/28. Winds howled early in the morn, tents shivvered, and rain slammed against the canvas. Temperatures dropped quickly, rain turned to freezing rain; then snow. Horses' manes and tails turned to ice.

MONDAY/30. Four inches of snow blanketed the ground but melted before dark and mud squished around horses' hooves.

Skies cleared. The soldiers built fires and held their wet uniforms close enough to dry. Some squeezed water from their blankets. Tentage dried. Jesse and John fed extra portions of corn and hay to their horses.

APRIL, 1863

SATURDAY/4. The company marched to a chaplain's tent and listened to his sermon.

SUNDAY/5. While soldiers slept and camp was calm on Easter Morning, Jesse saddled Sam and rode toward Goshen. He traveled beside the Orange and Alexander Railroad to Staunton where he stayed with a Davis family. From Staunton he rode to Charlottesville and stayed with a Head family.

THURSDAY/9. Jesse went to Hanover Junction.

FRIDAY/10. He got his medicine and started back.

SATURDAY/11. He reached Staunton. He rode to Goshen Depot; thence to camps. He told John, "I sure hope this medicine is enough to supply our camp. My trip was mighty unpleasant because I felt a fever coming over me and I coughed enough to shake Sam."

"I think the whole camp is sick. I've sort of got a fever." John coughed.

Days wore on. Horses ate all the corn. Hay was scarce. Days were fair but bitter cold. Grass failed to turn green. Feed ran out and the horses weakened. Jesse patted Sam's neck. "It hurts me to see you suffer this way. Perhaps we'll get a shipment of corn soon."

By month's end, distances shortened for riding picket. Passing through Virginia farmland, Jesse said to John, "Have you noticed how very little planting their farmers are doing?"

"Yeah. Soldiers crossing back and forth plus all the cold weather has put a stand-still on farming. Not only horses' rations but ours may run out."

Jesse and John exercised their horses. Jesse said, "Camp is too quiet."

"Maybe this is the quiet before a storm." John bit off a chew of tobacco.

MAY, 1863

SATURDAY/2. During company drill Jesse said, "I heard there's heavy cannonading towards Gordonsville."

John said, "That fits in with what I heard about the Yankees' General Joseph Hooker. You know he replaced General Burnside in January?"

"Yeah."

"The paper said that Hooker plans to use strategy plus an amassed strength of 134,000 men to annihilate General Lee. They've restructured units hoping to improve morale among the boys who suffered defeat after defeat. Poor things."

"John, this is a huge chess game. Our cavalry sees and interprets the plays. Their General Hooker placed General John Sedgwick in front of Fredericksburg to keep our General Lee there. Look at the Rappahannock on a map. The Union's main force under Hooker could move westward, cross the river upstream and their two wings together could crush our flanks. There's nothing to stop them from shoving their way straight down to Richmond." Jesse drew a line in the dirt with a stick.

"General Lee has already responded to that move." John picked-up the stick. "He left General Jubal Early's division there in front of Fredericksburg while he moved with the remaining Rebels into the wilderness."

MONDAY/4. Company C loaded their clothing on cars to be sent to Lexington. Jesse listened to a railroad clerk say, "There are rumors that fighting at Gordonsville is picking up."

Captain Henry announced, "Prepare to depart Rockbridge Baths and move to Gordonsville. I'll share this with you. General Hooker must have lost confidence in his main drive and ordered his forces to be defensive.

"General Lee pressed the offensive. He divided our forces further by sending General Stonewall Jackson's Corps on a round about march to Hooker's unprotected right flank. Late in the afternoon of 2, May, Jackson's boys dashed from the woods and dissolved the whole Union Corps.

"At approximately 9:00 P.M., a terrible thing happened. While General Jackson reconnoitered the Union lines a Rebel mistook who he was and shot. I don't know how seriously the general is wounded. General Jeb Stuart is temporary commander.

"On 3, May, General Stuart's soldiers smashed Hooker from the west. The Yankee wing crumpled and filed back to the Rappahannock. Personally General Lee led his army against Hooker from the south. So all of that went well.

"General Early had a rough time. While Generals Lee and Stuart fought Hooker General Sedgwick's men broke through Early's lines above Fredericksburg.

"General Stuart continued pressing Hooker's lines. After fighting at Salem Church near Chancellorsville, almost man-to-man, for two days the Union Wing reeled northward.

"With his troops General Lee moved to stop Sedgwick. Lee's very weary soldiers countermarched, aiming to wield a victorious blow to Hooker. He and his men had already retreated across the Rappahannock.

"That brings you up-to-date."

TUESDAY/5. Company C rode to Midway and camped.

WEDNESDAY/6. They continued to Waynesborough. Jesse ditched around his tent. "This rain has been heavy all day. The insides of my legs are rubbed raw."

"I've got a little salve you can use." John opened his saddle bag.

THURSDAY/7. The company marched and camped three miles south of Charlottesville.

FRIDAY/8. They passed through Charlottesville and camped eight miles east of said place.

SATURDAY/9. They marched and camped at Cobban Depot.

BRANDY STATION—THE LARGEST CAVALRY BATTLE—EVER

SUNDAY/10. They left for Orange Courthouse.

MONDAY/11. They camped near Orange Courthouse. Captain Henry announced, "General Hooker lost 17,278 men at Chancellorsville and General Lee lost 12,821. Yesterday General Stonewall Jackson died. Please bow your heads and pray in your own way for his family, along with all the others."

Jesse said, "I've studied General Jackson's tactics. His startling flank attacks brought smashing victories at Second Manassas and now Chancellorsville. I wonder if an era will pass away for General Lee."

FRIDAY/15. Company C left camps riding for Culpeper Courthouse ten mines farther north. They camped at Mitchell's Station.

SATURDAY/16. They continued riding to Culpeper.

SUNDAY/17. They camped near said place. For five days they cleaned their weapons, repaired their bridles and saddles, shod their horses, and reviewed battle techniques.

FRIDAY/22. They had a division review and sham fight.

JUNE, 1863

MONDAY/1. John said, "What do you think about all of this training we are doing? I think we are killing time."

"I expect a big fight soon." Jesse oiled a knife.

SUNDAY/7. Company C listened to Captain Henry. "Our cooks will fix up three day's rations. Be ready."

They rode to Brandy Station that day.

The earth thundered under the hooves of 18,000 war horses.

MONDAY/8. A radiant summer morning burst forth. Robert E. Lee, Commanding General of the Army of Northern Virginia, looked down from a knoll. Jesse and John, prancing their steeds, saluted the beloved general. Jesse said, "This grand review has about 10,000 horsemen and extends three miles."

"What a splendid sight. Look at General Lee's horse. They call him 'Traveler.' General Stuart knows how to organize a stirring martial display. I've got goose pimples all over me." John tightened his reins.

Captain Henry assembled Company C. "Boys, General Lee advised our cavalry that we'll be up long before dawn. We've got important business tomorrow. Y'all bed down early. Good night."

Jesse and John stretched out on the soft grass and pointed to individual bright stars. Jesse said, "I think General Lee decided to initiate a second invasion of the North for several reasons. Number one is our decisive victory at Chancellorsville. Two, we need to gain supplies. Three, hope for European support is fading. Four, striking a final blow at the Union is possible."

"You may be right." John yawned. "Tonight the important thing is Brandy Station. The Orange and Alexandria Railroad which links all these farms to the Army of Northern Virginia passes through here. Beverly's Ford and Kelly's Ford are two main crossings of the upper Rappahannock. We've ridden picket on her enough to know we can find sanctuary here, cover flank movements, and do reconnaissance missions."

"Isn't June a gentle month at Brandy? Smell the newly plowed earth. Tonight is cool and moist. Oh well, let's get some sleep." Jesse lay on his side.

"There's an early fog rolling into the low-lands. Have you received any letters from Sallie lately?"

"I got two the day we arrived at Culpeper."

TUESDAY/9. At daybreak the enemy advanced on Company C's pickets. By 6:00 A, M., they were regularly engaged. Union General Buford's cavalry splashed across the Rappahannock. Infantry and artillery support followed closely.

Confederate General John "Grumbles" Jones' Brigade roused and slung themselves into their saddles rushing headlong down the Beverly Ford Road. General Jones led the attack. He shouted, "Stop that Blue tide. Knock them off the river's banks."

Confederate artillery fired. Their guns were too close to Beverly Ford. A colonel yelled, "Form a line between Saint James Church and Gee House Hill."

Jesse said, "Oh, Boy. Look at our cannon tear up the earth beneath them."

General Jones sent a courier. "Ride to Fleetwood Heights it's about a mile and a half that way and tell General Stuart I need reinforcements on my right flank."

Company C of General Hampton's Brigade rode to a position near the Gee House.

Fighting progressed. Federals forced their way into open fields in front of Saint James Church. Horses pushed against horses. Sabres clanged against sabres, Sweat drenched horses and men. Blood streamed from animals and men alike. Many fell, mortally wounded.

A Yankees horse stumbled in front of Sam. John's panting horse lay kicking dirt. John tried to free himself from a stirrup. With his sabre drawn to deal death's blow another Yank rushed at John. Sam charged right. His feet entangled with the Yank's horse. The Yank's horse raised its head exposing its rider's bare chest. From a backhand movement Jesse's sabre cut the Yank from his horse.

Sounds of steel penetrating human flesh sickened and killed many riders. Eight hours passed.

Federal cavalry cut their way through several Rebel batteries. No support came to help the Yanks. Rebel horsemen nearly surrounded the men in blue. The frightened men fought their way out the same way they came in.

Union General David Gregg's column turned off and wound its way toward Brandy Station. Colonel Alfred Duffie's column moved from Stevensburg. Rebel gunners on Fleetwood Heights spotted Gregg's troops. The lone Rebel artillery piece opened fire and stopped Gregg's advance.

From Fleetwood Heights General Stuart sent orders to Generals Hampton and "Grumbles" Jones. "Press every available man to control this ridge northwest of Brandy Station. Federals are threatening."

Company C crested Fleetwood Heights. They met Yankee lines advancing up the slope from Brandy. Yankees prevailed for a while. Rebels attacked and counter attacked for another four hours.

A wild melee broke out. Pistols banged. Sabres clanged. Jesse heard a musket crack nearby. He felt an impact over his heart. He looked down. His eyes glared. Powder-burned, shredded cloth gaped on his chest. No blood oozed. Madge's arm dangled from what was once a pocket.

Jesse examined a small piece of tin around which Sallie Denton had made the doll. Within the doll's cotton stuffing rested a flattened minnie ball. Jesse grinned at John Robinson. "Sallie told me on the day I left home that Madge would bring me good luck."

"You owe your life to her." John stabbed a Yank.

Union columns recrossed the Rappahannock. At last today's fighting ended. Captain Henry reported to the company late that night. "General Stuart attempted to evaluate today. He said that this was a severe fight. He estimated the enemy losses to be twice as high as ours. We captured three abandoned Union cannons.

We're in control of the field; however, this site is so littered with casualties both human and animals, it is rendered unfit for human habitation. We'l guard it but not camp here.

"General Lee watched the battle from Barbour's House. His note to General Stuart stated something like this, 'The dispositions made by you to meet the strong attack of the enemy appear to have been judicious and well planned. Your troops were well and skillfully managed, and with few exceptions conducted themselves with marked gallantry.'

"Boys, you may have fought in the biggest and bloodiest cavalry battle in history. We'll move out and bed down."

WEDNESDAY/10. Rebel infantry columns marched northward. Jesse said, "This battle near Brandy didn't change General Lee's mind about a second movement into the North."

"I don't know about you but I'm ready to follow him to the ends of the earth." John Robinson frowned.

TUESDAY/16. Captain Henry reported, "On 14 and 15, June, General Lee's Army of Northern Virginia moved into Winchester and cleared out the Union Army. Rebels used the Shenandoah River to move across Maryland and into Pennsylvania."

WEDNESDAY/17. Company C galloped from Brandy Station and camped at Warrenton.

THURSDAY/18. Yankees approached within two miles of Warrenton. Company C met them and skirmished. The Yanks retreated.

FRIDAY/19. Company C left Warrenton and camped at Rexter's Crossroads.

SATURDAY/20. Rain poured all day. Company C rode out and took the front. Skirmishers fired back and forth. Rebels prevailed.

SUNDAY/21. Large numbers of Union Cavalry and infantry led by General Gregg struck Company C driving it back into the mountains. Without much fighting the company retreated to Upperville. Within fifteen minutes the company charged the Yanks four times. The Yanks took three prisoners, wounded Private Taylor severely, killed six horses and wounded several others.

MONDAY/22. Company C rode picket two miles south of Paris.

TUESDAY/23. They moved back to camps near Rexter's Crossroads. Here they received seven days' rations and left on a scout.

WEDNESDAY/24. They camped near New Salem.

THURSDAY/25. Company C began attacking Yankees at Thoroughfare Gap. After being shelled a little the Yanks retreated. Jesse camped at Buckland.

FRIDAY/26. They rode very hard toward Occoquan. Many, many horses gave out forcing the riders to stop. Captain Henry said, "We're within eight miles of Dumphries. Let's camp here. We'll feed our horses good rations, and they can rest."

SATURDAY/27. Early, Captain Henry ordered, "Company C, Mount up. We'll ride across Occoquan."

Near Fairfax Courthouse a scout yelled, "Yankees four hundred yards ahead. Camps are in the woods on our right."

"Columns of two. March." Captain Henry galloped ahead. "Charge."

The Yanks fled into Fairfax leaving many commissaries. Rebel cavalrymen laughed and talked gayly while they ate cheese and crackers, butter, and molasses.

"Company C. Mount up." Captain Henry waved his hand. Long shadows of trees rippled on the Potomac.

SUNDAY/28. At sun-up the last horseman crossed the river. Company C galloped toward Washington.

At Rockville, Maryland, only thirteen miles north and west of Washington, they encountered a small force. Rebel cavalry captured several hundred Yankees, two hundred wagons, and 1,500 mules and horses. The company set-up camp six miles north of Rockville.

MONDAY/29. They moved forward north. A band of Yankees met them at Westminster, Maryland. After a skirmish thirty Yanks surrendered and the others skedaddled. To rest Company C camped at Westminster.

Captain Henry said, "President Lincoln changes generals more than the Lord changes wind directions. General Lee's new opponent is General George Gordon Meade, general of the Army of the Potomac. Hooker resigned on 27, June."

TUESDAY/30. The Rebels rode north from Westminster toward Hanover, Pennsylvania. They met a large Yank force. Captain Henry ordered, "Follow me around this place."

Pressing every horse, they rode all night and passed through Jefferson.

NO WIN AT GETTYSBURG

JULY, 1863

WEDNESDAY/1. They rode north in the direction of Carlisle. Captain Henry announced, "General Ewell has a fight going to Gettysburg. At 11:00 P.M., Company C rides to join him."

THURSDAY/2. A full moon bathed the countryside, lighting the roadways. At 6:00 A.M. Company C commenced fighting.

During a lull Captain Henry said, "I wonder where General Ewell's command is? General Lee's message stated it is necessary to press the Yankees in order to secure the heights, Cemetery Hill, and Culp's Hill. Looks like General Ewell never advanced."

"It's going to be a long day." Jesse frowned.

At sunset Yanks attacked. Company C joined a charge which ran the Yanks back under cover of their artillery. Nine miles from Gettysburg Company C stopped.

General Lee told General Jeb Stuart, "Protect the army's left flank."

With Generals Jenkins and Chambliss' brigades General Stuart marched east on the York Road.

FRIDAY/3. Very heavy fighting broke-out at 4:00 A.M.

At 10:00 A.M., Company C rode a reconnoitering expedition. Five miles south of Hunterstown they found the Yankees. Immediately a fight commenced. General Fitz Lee's brigade and General Hampton's brigade, of which Jesse was a member, charged en masse. The engagement opened with a duel between Rebel horse artillery battery and two Federal batteries. Fighting swirled back and forth across cultivated fields between the Rummel and Lott farms north of the Hanover Road. Attacks followed counterattacks.

Rebel losses were slight; Yanks heavy. General Hampton suffered a sabre wound. Yanks wounded Dunlap, slightly wounded McDowell, and severely wounded Moore.

Artillery fire and flanking attacks drove back the 1st Virginia and Jeff Davis Legion. Captain Henry shouted, "General Stuart sent orders for us to withdraw to our original lines. On the opposite end between Big Round Top and the Emmitsburg Road the Yanks' cavalry suffered a bloody repulse. Follow me."

Late that night a visitor from General Lee's headquarters told them, "He announced that the greatest engagement ever fought in America has ended. It has been a sad, sad day for us. He praised the valor of our men but as he continued to speak, his emotions swelled and at the end he whispered, 'Too bad. Too bad. Oh, too bad.'

General Lee's emotions.

"All that remains for the Army of Northern Virginia now is a homeward journey."

SATURDAY/4. Company C didn't fight. They prepared for retreat. General Lee sent detailed departure times and order of march for each unit. About 1:00 P.M., a drenching rain swept in and stopped an hour later.

Seventeen miles long, the Rebel wagon train started. It moved through Cashtown and Greenwood. General Imboden's cavalry brigade escorted them.

Rebel infantry marched after dark, on the Hagerstown—Fairfield Road. General Stuart's other cavalry brigades rimmed the flanks and patrolled the rear.

Company C rode back to South Mountain Gaps and camped. Jesse said, "When the Gettysburg battle ended blood drenched every field."

"It made me sick." John Robinson sipped from his canteen.

MONDAY/6. Company C arrived in Williamsport. Yanks attacked. Rebels drove them back, inflicting great losses. The company remained there.

WEDNESDAY/8. Rain poured early in the morn. Jesse sat on a large root, tightened his shirt collar, and leaned against a tree trunk. "My eyelids are heavier than lead."

"Take a little sleep," John said. "The Potomac is rising so fast we can't cross it."

"That scares me. The Yanks will surely get us if we don't move." Jesse folded his arms.

"Mount up." Captain Henry sounded impatient. "Move out to Finchtown."

A rider met them at the edge of town. "General Lee's Army is all right. He entered Hagerstown yesterday. Many Federal infantry corps covered fifteen to twenty miles in the downpour in hot pursuit. Both armies have reported a combined list of 51,000 casualties. More bad news. General Ulysses Grant captured Vicksburg on 4, July.

"There goes our whole west. They just split us in two." Jesse toyed with his bridle reins.

THURSDAY/9. During the evening, Company C fought near Finchtown.

FRIDAY/10. Very early in the evening a fight commenced and lasted through the entire day. Jesse rode full speed hotly pursued by six riders. A Yank's minnie tore into Harden's hip. He yelled but didn't slow his horse.

At noon Rebel infantry came up and supported the cavalry.

SATURDAY/11. They lay at Finchtown skirmishing, shielded by a pitch-black night. Company C fell back to the Potomac.

SUNDAY/12. At daybreak they fell back some more. Jesse told John Robinson, "I expect a huge fight real soon."

The Potomac's waters subsided and engineers constructed a pontoon bridge.

MONDAY/13. Company C fell into line of battle and skirmished. All wagons crossed the river. With a squad Jesse rode back to cook. In a heavy rain most of the Rebel Army crossed the river during the night and re-entered Virginia.

TUESDAY/14. With the cavalry Jesse crossed at Williamsport, Maryland, at approximately 8:00 A.M.

Yankees struck. General Meade found out that General Lee moved his Army of Northern Virginia. Union cavalry divisions of John Buford and Judson Kilpatrick led this advance. Kilpatrick found Heth's troops at Falling Walters and charged with two squadrons.

John filled a bucket with mixed feed. "It's been exactly six weeks since General Lee marched his columns north."

"At the White House, President Lincoln told them that General Meade could have destroyed our army. He said, 'We had them in our grasp. We had only to stretch forth our hands and they were ours. And nothing I could do or say could make the army move.'" Jesse removed Sam's bits.

"General Meade's decision to attack our strongly entrenched army is too late. Our orderly retreat toward Virginia worked." John trimmed his horse's mane.

Four miles from Williamsport Jesse watched while the Rebel Army continued to fall back.

WEDNESDAY/15. The Jeff Davis Legion picketed along the Potomac.

THURSDAY/16. They continued to picket.

"I want some clean clothes. These can almost stand alone. There must have been a heap of clay along the river. I rattle every time I bend a joint." Jesse scratched dried mud from his face.

"Thank heaven you are uncommonly well and in fine spirits." John smiled.

"You're right."

FRIDAY/17. John Robinson's squad relieved Jesse's from picket duty. One of Jesse's boys pointed different positions. "There're twelve Yanks between us and Martinsburg, Maryland."

"Spread out." Jesse signaled. "Charge."

Rebel riders chased the Yankees at least six miles before they skedaddled into a woods and escaped.

SATURDAY/18. Jesse rode back into Martinsburg. While at the wagons he saw Henry. "I thought maybe you died after your gunshot wound at Gettysburg."

"Naw. I'm coming along all right. I expect the doctor will let me come back to the Legion next week."

"I'm sure glad you're all right. I've come to get some clean clothes. I'll step behind these bushes and change out. I'll leave what I have on for rags or they can burn 'em." Jesse took a knife from his pocket.

SUNDAY/19. Company C skirmished. The Yanks killed two men. Rebels killed two Yankees.

MONDAY/20. The company rode into camps near Martinsburg.

TUESDAY/21. Jesse rode picket. He and John Robinson found three catfish dangling from a fisherman's set-hooks. Jesse said, "I'm glad I sharpened my knife. We'll clean these and have a good dinner."

"I've got a couple of potatoes in my saddle bag. While we plank the fish, potatoes can bake in the coals. We can make believe that we have salt and pepper along with butter and lemon juice." John licked his lips and grinned.

Captain Henry assembled the company. "Boys, we received a report that the Yankees have us cut off. We'll ride up the river until we can go around them."

At 10 P.M., they dismounted and set up camp in a wheat field.

THURSDAY/23. At daylight Jesse rode a scout. He saw a lady scurrying about her kitchen. He held his musket ready and walked to the back porch. When the lady saw him she screamed.

"I'm not here to hurt you, Mam. You shouldn't be here by yourself."

"We thought the Confederate Army had all moved back to Virginia. My father and children rode into town to buy supplies." Her eyes darted to his and down to his rifle.

"Like I said, I'm not here to hurt you. All I want is something to fix breakfast with, eggs, fat-back, flour, and coffee." He lowered his rifle.

"I'll prepare a good breakfast for you. You can watch and be assured I'll not try to poison you. The Lord knows I'm frightened to death to be in the same house with a Confederate horseman."

Jesse ate a hearty breakfast. "I thank you, Mam. If I see any Yankee soldiers coming after me I'll find my way back and get you and your family."

"I won't say a word." She untied and retied her apron strings. "I promise you."

Company C found their regiment late in the day, near Darksville.

FRIDAY/24. They rode by Brucetown, Virginia, through Winchester, Newtown, Middletown, and Strasburg. They stopped to camp within five miles of said place.

SATURDAY/25. They rode through New Market, crossed over the Massanutten Mountain, continued through Luray, and camped nearby. Jesse sat in a dewberry patch and while he picked berries he listened to a band's sweet notes. His mind wafted back to the sweetest of by-gone days.

In his tent he lifted Madge, the rag doll, from his shirt pocket. Stained cotton showed through some loose threads. Jesse smiled. "You know, John, I wonder why a little girl such as Sallie Denton writes a horse-soldier, who is much older than she?"

"I'm sure she's learned a heap about the war during the last two years. Maybe she feels sorry for you; thinks you get lonesome for home." John stretched out on his blanket. "Maybe she loves you."

"She's too young." And Jesse fell asleep.

MONDAY/27. Company C galloped and walked over the Blue Ridge Mountains, passed through Sperryville, and camped nearby.

TUESDAY/28. They rode from Sperryville. Late in the day they passed through Culpeper and camped.

WEDNESDAY/29. Jesse was very hungry. The wagons rolled into camps hurriedly and he walked to them. Cooks served vegetable soup and passed out hard tack.

THURSDAY/30. Jesse rested. He washed clothes in a bucket of hot soapy water. He placed the wet clothes over a bush to dry. "John, don't you have a writing pen?"

"Yeah and I even have a few pieces of official Army paper. It's been a month or so since you wrote to Sallie."

"I know." Jesse looked at his dirty hands. "Be real still, John. Cast your eyes to the fork in that old oak tree yonder. Two of the prettiest half-grown coons I've ever seen are watching every move we're making. When they look at each other I believe they smile."

"They'd make some mighty fine eating. Get your gun." John stood motionless.

"They're too pretty to kill." Jesse clapped his hands and the coons scampered into the woods.

FRIDAY/31. In the early morning, Company C mounted up to move camps to a farm near Brandy Station. A picket reported. "The Yanks are advancing."

AUGUST, 1863

SATURDAY/1. At 7:00 A.M. Jesse told John, "I don't know about you but I'm a little drowsy and very hungry."

"I don't expect we'll get any sleep or food for a while. Sip from your canteen and pretend it's coffee." John dampened his kerchief and wiped his face.

At 11:00 A.M., and within one mile of Brandy, Yankees in overwhelming numbers, attacked the Rebel brigade. Company C fell back to Boot's House. Yanks charged the Rebel artillery.

"Company C, CHARGE." Captain Henry's voice shook the woods. The Rebel Yell thundered. Every horseman met the Yanks and routed them. Company C retired under deadly fire until they reached their infantry. Rebels drove the Yanks back.

Jesse felt Sam crumple into a heap of horseflesh. "Oh. No. They killed my most constant friend."

He crawled through sage while minnie balls whistled overhead. He found the wagons on Cedar Run. Quartermaster told him, "Company C had one man killed, one wounded, and one taken prisoner."

"We're lucky. You can add Sam to your list of casualties. The Yanks killed him. Sometimes I thought he understood the English language about as well as some of our soldiers."

SUNDAY/2. Jesse and four other riders galloped from camps. They rode from farm to farm looking for young, able-bodied men whom they might recruit for the Army of Northern Virginia. They also tried to buy horses from farmers.

One eighteen years old boy said, "My older brothers are already in the army; so I want to stay here until Pa and I get the crops in. I'll join y'all in late October."

The five horsemen stayed in Mount Millisses.

TUESDAY/4. They skedaddled on account of advancing Yanks. The horsemen passed through Orange Courthouse and spent the night three miles south of said place.

WEDNESDAY/5. Jesse was still on a lookout for recruits and pasture. He approached Barboursville. He thought: I've got to keep my eyes peeled for blue uniforms.

While passing through town he listened intently for the sound of Yankee accents along the streets. His eyes jumped from person to person.

THURSDAY/6. He passed over the mountains and stopped at a house near Orange. He knocked on the front door. A small old man opened it and smiled. Jesse said, "Sir, I'm looking for Rebel recruits."

"Our boys are already in the war. My wife and I are the only ones living here. My name is J. H. Lewis. It's almost dark. Can you spend the night with us? You look all tuckered out and arc probably hungry.

"Thank you, Sir. I'm both. My name is Jesse Sparkman and I'm from Cooksville, Mississippi. The Yanks killed my reg'lar horse a few days ago.

Can I stable this one? He might break his bridle and I'd hate to foot it back to camps."

"Oh, sure. Yankee soldiers stole all our horses."

FRIDAY/7. At daybreak Mr. Lewis knocked on Jesse's door. "You told me to awaken you. Ma has a big breakfast almost done."

"Thank you, Sir. Give me five minutes." Jesse stretched his arms.

Mr. Lewis held the horse's bridle while Jesse tightened the girths. "If you're ever back this way, stop by. We'd love to have you."

"Mr. Lewis, I might just do that. Y'all have been a blessing to me. I hope to meet your sons. I'm riding to Orange Courthouse today." Jesse spurred his horse and it reared up.

Late that afternoon, he crossed the Rapidan River by way of a cable bridge. He rode into Orange Courthouse. He saw a Confederate train stopped on a sidetrack. He found the engineer. "Are you stopping here all night?"

"Yeah. You lookin' for a place to sleep?"

"Yes, Sir. I need to be in Culpeper Courthouse tomorrow night. Our camps are close by there."

"I can't take you to Culpeper but you can sleep in the cars."

"Good. I'll leave my horse in that corral over yonder." Jesse turned his horse loose.

SATURDAY/8. He rode into Culpeper during the afternoon. He saw a cavalryman walk from a tavern. "Are camps at Brandy?"

"No, Sir. Ride out to near Stevensburg and look close on your right."

"All right. Thanks."

At camp he found the wagons and rode to the Quartermaster. "Have you seen John?"

"He's flyin' higher than a kite. Y'all are scheduled for furloughs in the next few days. Want some coffee?"

"You must have boiled this stuff all day." Jesse smiled. "Man, I'm hungry. What kind of food have you got?"

"I've got a fried chicken leg."

"That can't be beat."

FURLOUGH

SUNDAY/9. In the early morning Jesse and John saddle-soaped their leather. Jesse wiped his bridle. "Man, I'm anxious about getting a furlough. I wonder what things will be like at home."

"All we know about Cooksville is what they write in letters. I'm ready for some of my mother's cookin'." John replaced a stirrup.

MONDAY/10. They remained in camp. Jesse said, "Our boys are in high spirits today. If the Yankees value their lives they'd better not stand between us and Mississippi."

"If we could dangle those papers behind the Yank's lines, the war would be won in a day or two." John polished his boots.

"Ya hoo. YAH HOO!!" John waved furlough papers. "Company C Boys, attention while I call your names for furloughs."

John held the last furlough. "Jesse, this one is mine. I reckon you don't qualify."

"There's got to be some kind of mistake. Where's the company clerk?' Jesse kicked the ground. "Let me see that paper."

John Robinson's named filled the blank. A smile crept over his face as he carefully unbuttoned his shirt. "Oh. I forgot about putting this one aside. Let's see whose name appears on the line. It reads, 'First Lieutenant Jesse Roderick Sparkman.'"

"That's the way it better read." Jesse grabbed John by his throat. "What time do we leave for the cars?"

"At 2:00 A.M. 13, August."

THURSDAY/13. They left Culpeper. When they arrived in Gordonsville the train stopped. The train master announced, "You boys will have to lay off here until the 14th. The Exchange Hotel is down yonder a little. They built it in 1860; so it's like new. They've got fine cooks and you might consider spending your whole furlough there."

"You speak like a crazy man." Jesse smiled. "I haven't been home since the fall of '61."

"Well. I hope you have a wonderful time with your family. Are you married?"

"No, Sir. I'll think about that after the war." Jesse dragged his saddlebag from under the seat and walked to the car's platform.

"Look at the fresh paint on the hotel." John shifted his bags.

"Yeah, and I like the wide outside stairway between the middle columns on the second floor." Jesse looked up.

"With all the fighting that took place here you'd think this hotel would have been hit but I don't see a splintered board."

FRIDAY/14. In the morning's darkness they rode toward Richmond and arrived at 9:00. Jesse walked into a small tavern. "Everything is all right. This is a good bait of watermelon."

SATURDAY/15. At noon Jesse and some friends finished lunch at a Richmond restaurant. He said, "Paying three dollars a meal nearly kills me."

"I think the owners take advantage of military personnel. They know we're hungry for a good meal and will pay dearly." John counted off three Confederate Dollars. He stuffed the remainder in his shirt pocket.

At 4:00 P.M., the train's engine puffed black smoke. Cars lurched and couplings clanged. Jesse was on his way to Lynchburg, Virginia.

SUNDAY/16. At 5:00 A.M., the train rumbled out of Lynchburg; then pulled into Bristol's depot at 9:00. The trainmaster announced, "Before we can start for Knoxville, Tennessee, the train has got to have a new engine."

Jesse and John played checkers during a lay-over in Atlanta, Georgia. They played poker with several boys during a lay-over in a Montgomery, Alabama, depot. In Meridian, Mississippi, they looked at young ladies who walked about the station, sat on benches, twirled umbrellas, tapped their shoes against wooden oiled floors, and eyed the soldiers from behind fold-out fans. Now and then Jesse or John nudged the other with an elbow, pointed with a thumb, and mumbled. They both grinned. Meridian was their last lay-over.

SATURDAY/22. Jesse stepped from a surrey and walked the dusty lane to his house. "Hello, Mother . . . Papa. I spent nine days by train, traveling from Culpeper, Virginia, to Cooksville.

"We'll fix some catfish with all the trimmings. Samantha had good luck with her trotlines last night." His Mother smiled.

"I know you can't tell us all about the war, but what impressed you the most?" With his finger the older Sparkman pressed tobacco into a stained corncob pipe.

The cavalry used bugles for commands.
Can you imagine a drummer boy doing that?

Jesse sat in a large oak chair and rocked slowly. "I don't know. At the moment a thirteen year old drummer boy's story wraps up the war into a package for me. Many, many times I've heard the infantry's drums beat. I've heard our bugles blare.

"The drummer boy said that he, his mother and sister stood at the gate in front of their Virginia farm house while Confederate soldiers marched by. Chickens scurried about. His mother and sister gave cups of water to tired men. The boy heard a soldier say, 'Hey, Drummer Boy, how about a drum tap to get us in step?'"

"The thirteen year old listened to the drum beat and thought he could serve our cause by being a drummer. That night he slipped away from home, against his mother's wishes, and followed General Lee's Army. He heard them sing our song about Dixie Land.

"The army bivouaced and the boy searched campfire after campfire until he found a drummer boy. The thirteen year old learned to play rolls for assembly, attack, retreat, roll call, and mess call. He heard a soldier say, 'Don't he play good?'"

"His new friend warned him about battlefield confusion, noise, and smoke. He told him that there are times when men can't see or hear their colonel and they get lost. They hear the drum beat and it tells them what to do. Drummer boys have responsibility and duty.

"This thirteen year old drummer boy played and marched, crossing into Maryland, Pennsylvania, and the column came to Chambersburg. That night he heard the men say that they would fight at a little cross-roads town named Gettysburg.

"Next morning cannons Ba-Roomed in the distance. The boy's column marched behind Confederate lines at Gettysburg. During a break in the march the boy placed his drum on his back and told the sergeant about seeing some apples in a tree a short ways back. Behind the hill lay dead soldiers and horses. Shattered wagons, guns, food, and clothing sickened the bugle boy.

"Back in camp he asked his sergeant, 'Why are you here and why are you fighting?'

"I think the sergeant answered as most of us would. He said that his reasons for fighting keep changing. In the beginning he joined to have some fun and excitement, whip the Yankees in a few months, and return home. But those months have turned into two years. His pretty new uniform wore into a heap of rags draped across his back. He hadn't received pay in six months.

"Even though the sergeant didn't have a pretty uniform or money he told the drummer boy that he had pride, being a soldier in General Lee's Army of Northern Virginia.

"At 11:00 A.M. 3, July, his regiment's color bearer said that General Lee intended for them to bust through the center. His sergeant ordered a drum tap which moved them into a forward position. For two hours more cannons fired than ever experienced by the army.

"When the firing slackened a three star general ordered the drummer boy to sound assembly. The general told them that everything depended on them at the moment. He asked that each do his duty and plant Virginia's colors on the enemy's works today.

"Union artillery opened fire on the advancing gray ranks. The little drummer boy sensed that the beat of his drum marched men toward roaring guns. Men died because of his drum.

"The general ordered the long roll and shouted for the regiment to move forward. The drummer boy played harder and hoped to whip the Yankees. He yelled, 'Forward, forward, men.'

"At the end of an hour it was all over. The boy didn't know where the time went. His sergeant told him to play retreat. Rebels streamed back to Seminary Ridge.

"Back in the woods the drummer boy offered his canteen of water to wounded soldiers. He told one, 'We got whipped. I played as hard as I could but it wasn't enough. It was beautiful but horrible, too. They followed my drum.'

"The soldier told him, 'I know you want to go home, all of us do but you won't . . . not till it's over.'

"Every good military man feels that way."

Jesse's mother said, "I didn't realize that fourteen year old boys marched into battles."

"Yes, Mam. Both sides use drummer and bugle boys. Soldiers don't try to kill the boys. I need a wash-tub of water so I can bathe off some of this train smoke."

Dressed in clean starched civilian clothes, Jesse walked to the barn. He held a bridle. The leather was aged and cracks showed.

One of the reins was pieced together with wire. His father frowned. "We haven't been able to buy leather. You boys get it all. We make do with what we have."

"Do y'all have any chickens?" Jesse pointed to an empty pen.

"Some Yankees passed through a few days ago and took every one we had. Hungry soldiers do most anything for food. We caught some catfish. Your mother had some corn meal; so we'll have bread. The Yanks cleaned out the garden. We heard about some of the boys' stopping the war to swap coffee and tobacco across the rivers. We've got some coffee for you." Jesse's father smiled.

"The only horse we have is the old blind bay. Yanks took all the others. There hasn't been much fighting in Noxubee County but soldiers passed through, going for the fight at Vicksburg. That was a terrible loss for the Confederacy."

"I can handle the old bay. From what I heard we should have won Vicksburg." Jesse led the old horse to an open field.

NOVEMBER, 1863

MONDAY/2. A train ground to a stand-still at the Macon, Mississippi, depot. Its trainmaster waited for passengers to step off, baggage carts creaked under their weight, and the engine hissed after fresh water poured into Its tank. The trainmaster then looked toward the crowd and shouted, "All 'board"

Jesse lifted his saddle bags and walked to the train. He sat next to a window, opened it, and waved to his friends. The train inched from the depot while he watched the buildings fade into miniatures.

MONDAY/9. At 9:00 A.M., he arrived in Richmond, Virginia.

Before high-noon the train resumed its course. Hardly a mile out of the city limits Jesse heard a series of crashes. A jolt threw him from his seat. He stood and heard screams mixed with shouts.

"What happened?" He stepped from the aisle when the trainmaster rushed forward.

"For some reason we derailed. Saboteurs most likely. It's happening more and more."

Jesse stepped from his coach, looking toward the engine. Five cars lay on their sides. Passengers scurried from windows. He ran to the first car. A soldier lifted a small boy.

"Turn loose. I've got him. I have some antiseptic and bandages. Is that cut on his leg his biggest problem?" Jesse frowned.

"He's cut pretty deep. Glass hit him. I don't think he's hurt anywhere else. Don't let him try to walk. Stop that bleeding while I look for a medic." The soldier rushed away. The train's crew uncoupled each car and passengers, mostly service men; shoved them backwards away from the broken tracks. Crewman repaired the tracks and uprighted the cars. Hours passed; darkness approached while the train limped back into the station.

TUESDAY/10. At 6:00 A.M. Jesse walked from his barracks to the depot and boarded a train. He stepped from that train in Louisa, Virginia. He met with ten Confederate officers in a secret meeting room. They reviewed experiences related to attacks.

SUNDAY/15. He left for camp which he found five miles east of Orange County Courthouse.

FRIDAY/20. Company C drilled and participated in sham battles.

MONDAY/23. Captain Henry ordered, "Mount-up and head 'em out."

WEDNESDAY/25. They rode into camp near Talleysville.

THURSDAY/26. Captain Henry announced, "Boys, we leave this camp to meet the Yankees."

FRIDAY/27. At 12:00 noon they galloped on the plank road. Three miles east of Vidiersville they commenced a fight and got in some hot places, charging the Yanks behind the railroad.

SATURDAY/28. The weather changed into a very rainy day. Jesse told Captain Henry, "I expect an attack by the enemy. I've got that gut feeling."

"I don't know. We don't have any picket reports of their positions." Captain Henry pulled his coat collar closer around his neck.

SUNDAY/29. The Yanks advanced and forced Company C to skedaddle. "All right, Jesse, we may listen to your gut feelings. General Meade took the offensive, pushing southward almost to Culpeper. For several days the Yanks and Rebels maneuvered at Mini-Run. General Lee held an impregnable position."

MONDAY/30. Jesse stood in line of battle without any firing. Wet and cold, Jesse told the captain, "This is the most unpleasant day I ever saw."

"Boy, your memory is failing." Captain smiled.

DECEMBER, 1863

TUESDAY/1. The army didn't move. Jesse remained in camps one mile from the line of battle. Prudently General Meade withdrew to the Rapidan River.

WEDNESDAY/2. Yanks fell back across the river while Company C joined the Rebels' hot pursuit. Jesse's men captured a few stragglers and camped near Garmansford.

THURSDAY/3. They rode from camp, heading toward Hanover Junction.

FRIDAY/4. They continued to ride all day, reaching camps five miles east of Fredericks Hall. They received plenty of fodder for the underground railroad.

TUESDAY/8. Company C remained in camp. They moved one mile nearer the railroad. Weather turned cold and calm. They remained here.

SUNDAY/13. They rode toward Hamilton's Crossing.

WEDNESDAY/16. When they arrived Jesse told the Captain, "I haven't eaten for twenty-four hours."

"I know. We're all quite hungry. I think our cooks have some hard-tack and bacon. That beats nothing." Captain tightened his horse's girth.

FRIDAY/18. Rain set in.

SUNDAY/20. Furlough boys left camp. Jesse stood in line at the Quartermaster's. "You're telling that we get only one pound of beef and a quarter pound of bacon for the next four days?"

"That's it. Some folks are starving." Quartermaster handed a sack to Jesse. "These are very short rations but beat nothing."

THURSDAY/24. Jesse rode from camp with three men for whom he received orders to deliver to the provost guards at Fredericksburg. "You boys are charged with providing the enemy with information about our troop movements. You're spies for the Yanks. You'll ride your mount in front of me. No talking. And I'll kill the first one who makes a false move. I never have shot a man in the back but there's always a first."

The four men rode into the command post. A captain said, "Lieutenant Sparkman, deliver those men to cell block five. It's around the corner. Come back to me after you've turned them over to the guard. We'll get some food for you and a place to spend the night."

"Captain, how many Christmases have you spent away from home?"

"1861, 62, and now 63. Maybe we'll be home next year."

FRIDAY/25. Reveille sounded at the flagpole. Jesse groped around in the dark room, found, and lit a candle. At breakfast the captain yelled, "MERRY CHRISTMAS, Lieutenant Sparkman. You won't have to ride back to your camp today. You can help us with guard duty until 27, December."

"Do y'all serve turkey and dressin' for Christmas Dinner?" Jesse demolished two fried eggs.

"Maybe."

Late Christmas afternoon Jesse warmed his feet by placing them on a stone hearth in front of a large fireplace. He watched five drunk soldiers stagger to the flagpole. Four of them huddled. Suddenly they grabbed the fifth, tied his feet to the halyard, and hoisted him nearly half way up the pole. A colonel approached. Three stood at attention and saluted. Their partner with feet kicking recklessly was yanked up off the ground while their large friend dived.

"What the hell are y'all doing?" The colonel frowned.

"Celebrating, Sir. You want to join us?"

"Get those men off that flagpole."

SUNDAY/27. The sun set in a bank of clouds. Jesse rode into camp and reported his return.

MONDAY/28. A gentle rain began falling.

THURSDAY/31. Jesse told Captain Henry, "Well, Sir, 1863 ends and Company C rests from the ravages of war in Virginia."

"We're lucky to be here. Real lucky."

JANUARY, 1864

FRIDAY/1. "HAPPY NEW YEAR. Joe. Open your eyes and look at the golden sunrise." Jesse jerked the blankets. Blood saturated Joe Barnes' long winter underwear near his right knee. His teeth clattered uncontrollably.

"I'm sorry you saw this knee. A minnie ripped it open when we skirmished a few days after we left Orange Courthouse. I think it got infected but might heal up." Joe wrapped a rag around his knee tightly.

"It ain't gonna heal. Get up. I'm taking you to the doctor. Have you ever watched him cut off a leg?" Jesse folded Joe's blankets.

"That's what I'm scared of."

"They can treat you at Fredericksburg Hospital and you'll be well pretty soon. You're lucky we're this close. My God, may the first day of January next find us at home living amid peace and prosperity."

"That's easy for you to say. You're having a tolerable good time here in winter quarters. You can play poker and checkers in your spare time. I'm plain scared of hospitals." Joe tossed a deck of playing cards onto his saddle bag.

"I think the doctor will let me stay with you until you begin to heal."

"Okay. Let's go."

Every morning for the next two weeks Jesse heard their bugle-boy blast out reveille at 5:00 A.M. His blankets were snuggled up around his neck and shoulders. Firewood was scarce. He splashed near-freezing water on his face, shivvered while he quickly put on his uniform, and grunted, tugging at a boot. "These things are stiff."

In the corral, horses bowed their backs. Men laughed, greeted each other, whistled at their horses, bridled, and saddled them.

At eight o'clock Jesse heard Captain shout, "Fall In."

Each day the division formed two teams, one red; one blue. They simulated battles. Drill, drill, drill until 4:00 P.M. "Your weapons are grimy. Clean and oil them for inspection tomorrow morning.

Saddle-soap your bridles and saddles. All of you would be dead by now if you keep on allowing the enemy at your flanks. Straighten up. No questions."

The men muttered beneath their breath, some lit lanterns in the cabin, and played poker before going to bed.

SATURDAY/16. Jesse rode picket duty at Germanna Ford. This duty continued.

WEDNESDAY/20. Jesse rode toward camp.

THURSDAY/21. Late in the afternoon while in the cabin, he rubbed neatsfoot oil into his boots. Suddenly one of the boys whispered from an open window, "A hog o'possum and two smaller ones are marching into camp. Let's form a circle around them, rush in, and catch 'em. Cookie can fix a 'possum dinner tomorrow."

"Three coons should be marching in. They're not nearly as greasy as 'possums." Jesse stuffed his feet into shiny boots.

The 'possums raced back and forth within the circle. One broke through and escaped. Two boys pounced upon the others and killed them with knives

"We're living high and having a jolly good time." Jesse skinned one 'possum. "We've got oysters for supper and breakfast."

"And now 'possum for dinner." Captain sheathed his knife.

SUNDAY/24. Jesse drew sugar and coffee. He yelled, "Shut the door, Becca. People who haven't walked in our boots don't understand. They don't realize that one-half spoonful of sugar and a cup of coffee to the man are no little things."

"A cup of coffee is something to be happy about." Quartermaster stirred in his sugar and sipped.

TUESDAY/26. Jesse marched alone at the camp's secret entrance. At midnight his replacement, John, whispered the password. "Café Vienna."

"All is well, John. It's a quiet cold January night." Jesse adjusted his rifle.

"I've been in the army six days and this is the first supper I've eaten. I knew it would be hard but I thought cooks fixed suppers of some sort even if only hard tack."

"Nothing is certain. You may spend days with only the food you kill or steal. You'll learn in a hurry to eat whenever and whatever you can." Jesse walked toward his cabin. "I think you'll find the next few days in camp to be quiet with regular meals."

FEBRUARY, 1864

SUNDAY/7. At daybreak Captain announced, "Company C has orders to be ready to ride at a moment's warning. Yankees have crossed the Rappahannock in full force."

At 10:00 A.M. Company C was ready for marching.

At 12:00 Noon they marched over to General Young's Headquarters.

At 3:00 P.M. left for picket.

MONDAY/8. They reached picket post at 3:00 A.M. Jesse said, "Yankees all gone back."

SATURDAY/13. Company C remained on picket. A soldier came into camp walking on his hands and knees. A Yankee saddle covered his back; stirrups dragged along. A group of laughing soldiers followed.

"Hey. What's going on with you boys?" Jesse lifted the saddle. "How'd you get this fine piece of Yankee equipment?"

"Sleight-o-hand. Sleight-o-hand. Don't ask no questions. Does the Lieutenant want this lovely gift or not?" A soldier grinned.

"I'll take it. Thanks. Listen to all those drums across the river. Plenty of Yankees are quite close. Be ready to saddle up." Jesse smiled as he walked away holding the saddle.

WEDNESDAY/17. The weather turned very cold.

THURSDAY/18. Ice measured four inches thick on ponds.

SUNDAY/21. Jesse wrote home. "Oh, lonesome I am. My mind is often wafted back to by-gone days. Yes, to those blissful moments spent among dear relatives and friends. Those pleasures are mixed up with an unexpressable degree of sentiment, of joy passed, and of pleasures gone forever; gone, but oh, I look forward and hope for a glorious future."

FRIDAY/26. A cook told Jesse, "Our rations are quite short; so we're gonna have some hungry boys."

"I heard about y'all making soup twice from the same soup bones." Jesse stirred a pot.

"Yes, Sir, and the second time, we cut the bones into small pieces." Cookie wiped his hands on a rag.

"I don't like to complain but one quarter pound of beef or other meat per day is not enough."

"No, Sir. We have to stretch our rations equally among the troops."

"We're willing to fight on even if we don't get anything but bread. We will fight so long as we are able to strike a deadly blow to the Yanks." Jesse stared into the black pot.

SUNDAY/28. Company C mounted their horses and rode from camps to picket. They rode into Germanna Ford at 3:00 P.M. A rider met them and reported, "Plenty of Yankees are about. Expect and be ready for an attack."

Yanks attacked and captured several Rebel pickets at 11:00 P.M.

MONDAY/29. The Yank's action was reported to the other pickets.

Immediately after receiving news that Union General Hugh J. Kilpatrick commanded—in person—some 3,000 cavalry and six pieces of artillery, Company C fell back. Jesse said, "I hope the Yanks are as miserable in these blasts of cold wind as I am."

Captain secured the top button of his coat. "If this wind would die-down a little I'd be more comfortable. We've got to expect the enemy by the hour now. One slow hour at a time."

On foot at 3:00 P.M. the Yanks attacked the Rebel pickets. Company C fought back.

"General Kilpatrick, with his 4,000 cavalrymen, left the Union Army's camps along the Rapidan River and rode southeast. His raiders reached Spotsylvania Courthouse in the wee hours of this morning." Captain spurred his horse.

"Our boys are falling back with some confusion." Jesse rode alongside the Captain.

"This is as bad as the home stretch. Our dictator is get up and get, boys. The fastest leads. You and I must ride faster. Are you ready?" Captain looked into Jesse's sparkling eyes.

"READY." Jesse leaned forward in his saddle.

MARCH, 1864

WEDNESDAY/2. Company C took their picket post on the Rappidan. "Captain, have any of our pickets spotted General Kilpatrick?"

"Yeah. They reported that a 500-man detachment led by a Colonel Ulric Dahlgren veered south from Spotsylvania with orders to cross the James River, hook back, and attack Richmond from the south. Kilpatrick will strike from the north.

"Yesterday, some 500 of our boys, manning Richmond's outer fortifications forced General Kilpatrick to flinch. He pulled his Yanks back and waited for dark. Some Rebel troopers messed-up his plans. They fought him in his camps. The general dropped his mission and headed for Union lines farther south."

"What happened to Dahlgren?" Jesse sipped hot coffee.

"Don't know yet."

THURSDAY/3. Jesse rode picket in thick undergrowth near the river. "There's one good thing about today. The weather's pleasant."

When the sun sank behind the trees and Company C found no trace of Yank's movements they formed for camps. After dark, Captain talked with Jesse, "You asked about Colonel Dahlgren. The rumor is he's dead."

"You're kidding." Jesse smiled.

"Naw. We know the James River is rain choked. The Colonel couldn't cross; so he led his men against Richmond, from the west. Our Home Guards drove them off. His detachment rode north around Richmond; then south to find General Kilpatrick. Along with approximately 100 men he got cut off from his main force.

"Between King and Queen Courthouse and King William Courthouse, Rebel cavalry ambushed the small band. They killed the Colonel and captured his men last night."

"Looking at my map, that placed them north and east of Richmond." Jesse folded his chart and placed it in his saddlebag.

"There's another interesting rumor about Colonel Dahlgren. Our ambushers found papers signed by the colonel that outlined plans to burn Richmond and kill President Davis, along with his staff."

"That's just about a kiss of death for those captured raiders. They should be shot on the capitol's lawn." Jesse removed and looked at his gloves.

FRIDAY/4. At night Yanks fired on Rebel pickets. "What time is it."

"Nine o'clock. Return their fire. They think we are crossing the river." Captain rode throughout his troops.

"Captain, I'm taking one man with me and report to Elys Ford. Our firing caused some confusion." Jesse turned his horse and rode down stream.

"Watch out, Lieutenant. Those bursts on our left are Yankees'." The rider stopped his horse.

"Yeah, but they're across the river. They can't see us. Come on."

Jesse rode inside the wood's edge.

"Did you hear that? Some bullets whistled over our heads." The rider stopped again.

"Don't worry. You're just seeing and hearing a great many jack-o-lanterns. You'll get used to it."

SUNDAY/6. At daylight John rode to Jesse's picket station. "I'm relieving you for a few days."

"I'm very glad because I am worn out and getting careless. We haven't found any trace of Yanks." Jesse mounted his horse.

"With this fine weather our pickets have been able to follow General Kilpatrick real close. He moved to the Peninsula." John lit his corncob pipe.

"Why would he move to the Peninsula?"

"Don't know."

Jesse rode into camps at 9:00 A.M. A cook handed a plate of bread and scrambled eggs to him.

WEDNESDAY/9. At assembly Captain announced, "Today Union General Grant moves east to take over command of all Federal Armies. His strategy is brutal. He wages total war. His Federal forces have plowed ahead in unrelenting drives applying pressure on all points of our Confederacy. I'm certain General Grant reasons that our depleted armies can't defend every sector successfully. And he's probably right. He calls it a war of attrition."

Jesse broke in, "It's really a war of sledgehammer tactics. He intends to knock away our ability to fight."

SATURDAY/12. With four men Jesse rode from camps to establish a line of real courses from headquarters to Port Royal, south and east of Fredericksburg.

SUNDAY/13. Riding near Port Royal, Jesse said, "Boys, look over yonder to our left. Can y'all see that big rabbit?"

"Yeah, and he ain't scared of us one bit. He's probably watched Yankees parade back and forth on those fields." Henry spurred his horse.

"This is certainly a beautiful Sabbath morning. All nature seems to be smiling down on us. The scenery around Port Royal is so pretty." Jesse galloped alongside Henry.

MONDAY/14. Jesse said, "I see a farmer behind that house, working on a plough. Let's find out if he's seen our wagons."

"Hello. Are you boys lost? I'm Kelon Rowe." He tightened a bolt.

"No, Sir." Jesse introduced himself and the others. "We are looking for our wagons and wondered if you saw them pass."

"I sure did. Early this morning, they were headed toward the lower port. You should be there about mid-afternoon. Mrs. Rowe is fixing dinner. If y'all will stop long enough, we'd be happy to have you eat with us."

"That's mighty kind of y'all. We are a bit hungry." Jesse smiled and unmounted. "Can I hold your plow while you finish tightening that bolt?"

"Sure. Then I'll go tell Mama to put on more plates. She's the best cook in these parts."

Mr. Rowe pulled a bucket of water from a well on the back porch. "You boys wash your faces and hands. I'll be right back."

While Jesse washed his face, a shapely young lady strolled up to him. "Excuse me, but Daddy told me to bring a bucket of hot water for y'all to use."

"This is a real treat. It's been a spell since we used hot water." Jesse looked at the lady's pearly white teeth and spilled water all over himself.

"Watch out." Her eyes twinkled.

"I, uh, excuse me for staring at you but you remind me of a little girl back in Mississippi." Jesse's face crimsoned. "Her name is Sallie Belle."

"Mine is Belle." She wiped the spilled water with a towel.

Mrs. Rowe served fried chicken, potatoes covered with gravy, creamed corn, peas, biscuits and cooled milk. The riders scraped their plates with biscuits.

"We hate to eat and run but we need to be at the lower port by evening." Jesse smiled at Belle. "Perhaps we'll ride this way again."

"And spend the night with us?" Belle's eyes fluttered.

"We'll see." Jesse turned his horse and rode away. He and his men camped near the wagons.

One of the men said, "Their fodder, oats, and corn are a glimmering sight for our horses."

"Maybe we can stay here a few days to build-up our horses." Jesse walked to his tent.

TUESDAY/15. The weather turned quite cold at the Cavalry Academy. At supper Jesse told his men, "I feel joyful over the prospect of being relieved from duty."

"Me, too." One smiled.

SATURDAY/19. Jesse and his four men received orders, relieving them of courier duty.

SUNDAY/20. They rode from Hamilton Springs for Chesterfield.

After dinner Jesse patted his stomach. "One thing is certain. I ate a good quantity of Ol' Tom."

APRIL, 1864

FRIDAY/1. April Fools' Day brought quite a lively time in camps. Several April Fools started a sham fight. Cooks prepared fine "Tom Thumbs" for dinner. One boy reported to Jesse, "I shot and killed John."

"You're joking. Go tell the cooks that all of us who partook highly appreciated the delicious essence."

TUESDAY/5. Weather turned very unpleasant. In a chilled cabin a violinist played his instrument. Jesse said to the captain, "Oh, those sweet notes cause my mind to turn to beautiful reminiscences of days by-gone. I feel quite sentimental and melancholy."

"I know how you feel I think." Captain loosened his boots. "I wish I could be home with loved ones tonight."

"This is quite a monotonous life we are having. I prefer an active campaign. What we have is a close resemblance to when we first came out." Jesse tapped a foot in rhythm with the violin.

"We'll have an active campaign soon." Captain frowned.

SUNDAY/10. Jesse wrote. "Dear Mother, I have just heard a good sermon. Oh, may the prayers of the many thousands that are bowing before the Maker be the cause of a speedy peace and let us return home as citizens once more. Has not enough of our sunny South been devastated? Are there not enough widows and fatherless children? President Davis said, 'May we be let alone is all we ask.'"

That night he wrote in his journal, "Oh, may this be a blessed day for our having been convinced fully, years ago, that we should be prepared to die at any moment. I will, this day ask God's blessings. Oh, may Thou lead me from this day on and may I become a true Christian. May, oh may, I never be tempted by the thousands of temptations that attend this cruel war. Oh, may I be guided by Thy fostering hand."

HORRORS OF THIS WAR

THURSDAY/14. Jesse entered in his journal, "Oh, the horrors of this war. What pencil portrays them? Surely a just God will punish those northern fanatics for the misery and death they are spreading over our land. Yes, a day of retribution must come, a day when they shall be made to feel the curse of their own evil doing. Sometimes I wish the Earth might engulf them as the wicked were engulfed in the Red Sea. My whole desire is that soon may we enjoy a speedy peace.

"While I am writing the sun is casting its penetrating rays over the western horizon. A sacred turtle dove is finishing her song for a night's rest amid the green foliage of Virginia's enchanting forests. Ah, I hear joyful shouts of my fellow-soldiers playing town ball. How little they are thinking of how soon the hands of this cruel war may lay them low, in their last resting place forever. I am here sitting on a grassy mound; nearby a shiny stream flows over its pebbled bed. But oh, are my mind and heart there? No, No. I am thinking about loved ones at home—far, far away. May I soon see them in peace."

SUNDAY/17. At midnight Jesse went on guard duty. He wrote in his journal, "I feel sentimental. All is calm and serene as a summer's morn and nothing to be heard save the sentinel's tread, marching from post to post, keeping watch while thousands sleep unmolested.

I cast my eyes to the blue expanse above. There I see the moon and its thousands of shining worlds. Every ray seems to penetrate to the farthest part of this great galaxy."

TUESDAY/26. Company C rode toward the front from Chesterfield. They camped on Rockburg Farm.

WEDNESDAY/27. They arrived in Hamilton Springs and pitched camp in regular order.

SATURDAY/30. Jesse and Captain tethered their horses. The sun shone brightly. Jesse said, "I can almost see the grass and trees turn green. Our horses need some good grazing."

Captain plucked a blade of grass and nibbled on the stem. "Surely the great struggle we've been expecting is on the brink of advancing. Our very hard duty at Chesterfield should prepare us for it."

MAY, 1864

TUESDAY/3. Amid Virginia's enchanting foliage skirting the Rapidan River, Captain rode to Jesse's side. "General Grant with approximately 118,000 Yankees crossed the river. Our pickets spotted them."

"The great struggle, as you call it, which may boggle our minds has begun. Only time will reveal our fate." Jesse looked between his horse's ears.

"A study of intelligence unfolds General Grant's strategy. He began three separate offensives at the same time. General Franz Sigel moved 6,000 troops into the Shenandoah Valley. General Benjaman F. Butts marched 36,000 from Fort Monroe up the Peninsula. It looks as if Grant plans to place his troops between General Lee's 60,000 Rebels and Richmond." Smoke drifted from Captain's pipe.

"I can understand why the Yankees want to control the valley. Much of our food is raised in its plush soil. Why is he moving up the Peninsula?"

"I don't know."

WEDNESDAY/4. The cavalry left Hamilton Springs and rode toward Spotsylvania Depot.

THURSDAY/5. When they approached Chancellorsville, Jesse stopped his horse. "I hear cannonading."

"At four o'clock we are ordered to ride picket through Spotsylvania Courthouse." Captain spurred his horse.

The Wilderness, an area of dense bramble and trees, lay west of Fredericksburg. The snare entangled Generals Lee and Grant's armies. Nature's strength held firmly. Captain galloped his horse back and forth along the edge. "It's no use, the density prevents any entrance and then movement of cavalry and artillery."

Bugles blared, "ATTACK."

"Dismount." Captain led the way into the battle zone. Jesse looked at trees, lopped and scarred by balls and shells. Here and there lay moldy blankets, rusty guns, ammunition boxes, cracker boxes, and small bone heaps, covered with rottened uniforms, too weather beaten to distinguish from which army the soldier had been missing.

Trudging along, inching down a small ridge, Captain said, "I may not have the correct information but I was told that out there is the lane, is where General Jack's own man shot him."

"Look on that rise just this side of those trees." A Rebel voice screamed. "Yanks by the thousands. Lined up on their colors."

"Far as my eyes can see up the pike, Yanks are massed lying down." Jesse leaned forward in his saddle.

Both armies attacked and counterattacked. Organization disintegrated when flames roared, sounding similar to a train through the undergrowth, consuming men who couldn't get out of it uncontrolled madness.

Continuously on foot, Jesse fought in the Wilderness.

FRIDAY/6. He crawled back to his tethered horse. He rode from Spotsylvania Courthouse toward Bethany Church at 6:00 P.M.

SATURDAY/7. At daylight he was in his saddle ready to march. Company C rode from Bethany Church at six o'clock, ordered to Shady Grove.

After they stopped to rest their horses in a pasture Captain announced, "Headquarters reported that General Grant lost 17,666 men. The Army of Northern Virginnia, 11,400. Grant stopped the fight and moved his army easterly trying to turn our right flank. Our dwindled mass raced Grant to Spotsylvania Courthouse and won. There has been some skirmishing with heavy cannonading along the lines. Reports say we are all right. Be ready to march in the direction of Spotsylvania Courthouse in the morning at five o'clock."

SUNDAY/8. One mile from Shady Grove a picket found the Yankee's cavalry. At 11:00 A.M. Company C advanced. They heard Captain's command, "Charge."

Company C drove the Yankees at least a mile without much opposition. Yankees made a stand. Rebels charged and blue uniforms ran back to their infantry.

At that time Yankees charged and drove Company C back with some loss. Sergeant Creekmore was missing.

MONDAY/9. General Longstreet's Corps passed. General Ewell's Corps followed.

"Be quiet and listen." Jesse turned around. "I hear some musket firing in the direction of Spotsylvania Courthouse."

"You're right. Let's prepare the boys to move out." Captain lifted his saddle.

"Yeah."

At 2:00 P.M. Captain shouted, "Company C. Mount up."

They left Shady Grove riding for Wait's Shop. Soon the Yankees attacked in large force. Rebels skedaddled.

Lee's Army of Northern Virginia waited, entrenched at Spotsylvania Courthouse. Grant's forces marched. The two clashed.

During a halt in the Wilderness battle Grant's staff lifted pews from Bethesda Church and placed them in a horseshoe formation in the church yard. A picket inched close enough to see the whites in Yankee eyes. In the spring breeze heavy winter uniforms looked hot. An armed guard stood around this carefully selected staff.

General Grant's lips moved while he wrote orders and handed them to individuals. Some frowned while they read. The picket listened to Grant say, "Do you understand my plans?"

He waited. "Do you know your assignments? Any questions?"

YANKS KILLED GENERAL STUART

T UESDAY/10. General Grant's forces struck. His and General Lee's armies fought harshly, brutally, intermittently. Yanks attacked Company C and drove them back to the Orange and Spotsylvania Road. A minnie-ball studded into the hip of Jesse's horse.

When at a safe distance, Jesse stopped and examined the wound. A shallow cut caused very little blood to ooze.

Re-enforcements joined the Rebels. They drove Yankees back across the river. Jesse shouted, "Shoot those swimmers."

WEDNESDAY/11. Jesse rode picket two miles from camps. Late in the afternoon boys chose sides and played town-ball. Cooks served plenty to eat for supper.

"Bad news." Captain placed his hat over his heart. "We suffered a most crucial loss. A Yankee mortally wounded General Jeb Stuart today during a cavalry fight at Yellow Tavern."

"A year ago we lost General Stonewall Jackson and today we lost our cavalry's fearless General." Jesse bowed his head.

THURSDAY/12. Jesse remained in camps. He cleaned and oiled his weapons. At 3:00 P.M., Captain called, "Company C. ATTENTION. Fighting on the lines is very heavy. Slaughter is great on the enemy. The glorious report is we repulsed the enemy at every charge. Temporarily Yankees overran a sector of General Lee's lines at a place they're calling 'Bloody Angle.' Many of our men got cut and killed by bayonets during hand-to-hand combat. This must have been some of the bloodiest fighting thus far."

FRIDAY/13. At 1:30 A.M. Captain shouted, "Company C, Mount up."

Men scurried in darkness, saddled horses and wiped their eyes. In assembly they listened. "Fighting continued all night. Fourteen hours."

SATURDAY/14. "It's 2:00 A.M. now. We're riding for our breastworks on the left flank. Move out."

In pouring down rain Jesse tightened his coat collar around his neck.

"Yesterday, General Grant sent four divisions against our salient. The outward bulge at the center was so large the boys called it 'Mule Shoe.' The Yanks can't break it. Fighting for twenty hours in this rain is tough." Captain wiped his face.

Company C occupied their position in breast-works. Lee's Rebel Army moved to the right.

SUNDAY/15. Jesse crossed to the north side of the Potomac River going on a scout. Paraphernalia from the Army of the Potomac covered the countryside.

MONDAY/16. Jesse started on a scout riding near the Rappahannock River.

TUESDAY/17. Jesse left on a scout. His boys stopped to graze their horses near Martin's Ford. They camped five miles north of Coccoon Ford. Their horses nibbled on very fine grass.

WEDNESDAY/18. After crossing the Rappahannock, cavalry camped four miles north of Falmouth, Virginia. They found the Yanks. Captain said, "After studying their numbers, I believe they're too strong for us to attack."

THURSDAY/19. Riding for their camps, Company C rode into Yellow Chapel Church grounds at 9:00 A.M. A neat lady stepped out of the church. "My name is Mrs. Irving and we have enough fresh crackers and butter if you boys want refreshments."

"Mam, you're a sight for sore eyes. We can eat anything." Jesse helped with serving and set a bucket of water on the porch.

A picket reported "Yanks on the road a quarter mile away."

"Mount up," Captain waved his hand.

The boys captured 95 Yanks; then rode on to Ellis Ford and camped.

FRIDAY/20. Company C spurred their horses toward the Rappahannock at Germansford. Lee's Army of Northern Virginia sealed their works at the salient's base where on 18 and 19, May, General Grant failed to break the new line. Locating their wagons, Company C camped on the Orange and Spotsylvania Road.

General Grant slipped around Lee's right, marching toward Hanover Junction, a Rebel rail and supply hub, south of the North Anna River.

SATURDAY/21. Company C left their wagons and rode for Milford. Two miles north of Milford they met and joined their army to skirmish the Yanks.

General Lee ordered a fortified convex V-shaped line with its apex on the North Anna River. Grant couldn't attack effectively. The shape of Lee's line forced Grant to split up his army into halves divided by Rebel works and the river.

SUNDAY/22. Rebels fell back. Company C camped on the North Anna River two miles from Hanover Junction.

MONDAY/23. Yanks advanced on the Rebels early. They skirmished until 4:00 P.M. Rebels crossed the North Anna and camped at Robinson Springs.

TUESDAY/24. Company C galloped for their left flank on Middle River. At 12:00, noon, Jesse barely finished his breast works when Yankees came and skirmished. Jesse went on picket at Anderson Mills.

While Jesse and Captain rode side-by-side, Jesse said, "The clear skies and soft breeze touch a soldier's heart. This kind of day makes my mind flee back to sweet reminiscences of by-gone days."

"Don't dwell on home. After the skirmishes on 23, May, the Yankees sidestepped General Lee and moved southeast toward Richmond. It's a long way to this war's end. We lost General Stuart on 12, May, and the Yanks lost their General Sedgwick on 9, May." Captain rested his hand on his sabre.

"General Wade Hampton took General Stuart's place. I hope General Hampton works out."

THURSDAY/26. Company C remained in camps for the first time in twenty-two days.

FRIDAY/27. The Army of Northern Virginia fell back. General A.P. Hill's Corps passed the cavalry. Jesse saw a good many of his friends. Company C camped near South Anna River.

SATURDAY/28. They awakened and marched toward Richmond. They camped on Taylor's Farm, twelve miles north of Richmond.

SUNDAY/29. The cavalry left camps and rode almost to Hanover Courthouse. They met Yankees and had some picket firing.

MONDAY/30. Company C camped near Hanover Courthouse.

TUESDAY/31. Jesse rode picket two miles above Hanover.

JUNE, 1864

WEDNESDAY/1. Jesse rode back to Taylor's Farm and camped. Coffee perked in a small blue pot. Captain stirred some coals. Names of 55,000 Yanks inked the pages of General Grant's Army of the Potomac as casualties. They nearly equaled the entire number of men General Lee had when his Army of Northern Virginia began this campaign."

Jesse said, "I saw in a paper that General Grant remained unmoved at those staggering figures. He considered the sacrifices necessary and worthwhile. He proposes to move his army south and east. The paper quoted him, 'I propose to fight it out on this line if it takes all summer.'"

"We'll see." Captain poured a cup of coffee.

FRIDAY/3. Company C rode for Cold Harbor, where Lee and Grant's armies already engaged in a brutal battle. Union troops assaulted Lee's lines fourteen times. Every assault failed, because Rebels dug-in on 1 and 2, June, awaiting Grant's attack.

Returning to Attes Depot, Jesse shivvered. "It gives me goose-bumps to see hundreds of Yanks unattended on the battlefield. Many have been there more than a day. Don't you know the broiling sun intensifies their suffering?"

"General Grant doesn't care. Our troops estimated more than 7,200 Yankees fell dead or wounded within a half hour's fighting."

Captain wiped sweat.

SUNDAY/5. Jesse rode picket. "You know, Captain, I wish I could be home and see loved ones."

"Aw, Jesse, you want to see how grown-up Sallie is." Captain smiled.

"She certainly has been faithful about writing letters. She's too young for me to court. Look, there goes the foot squad." Later Jesse rode into camps and found a friend, Henry.

MONDAY/6. Jesse remained in camps near Medan Bridge.

THURSDAY/9. A Yank raiding party sneaked into camp. A sentry spotted them, sounded an alarm, and Company C chased the raiders.

FRIDAY/10. Company C rode through Beaver Dam, Bumpus, and Louisa Courthouse. They stalked Yankee forces traveling in a direction which led to Gordonsville.

SATURDAY/11. Company C rode into Trevilians Depot. Yankees attacked early and the fight lasted all day. Company C lost five men, missing and wounded.

SUNDAY/12. Jesse fought hard. Corporal Harris, who was close-by screamed, "Oh. My leg."

Jesse saw blood spurting from Corporal's left boot. "I'll come along your right side. Get on my horse. I'll help you. We've got to stop that blood. While I come around tear off a strip of your shirttail."

In camps the doctor handed a minnie-ball to Corporal. "Drink this whiskey and when I tell you to, bite this bullet as hard as you can. The only way to save your life is for you to lose your leg."

Corporal passed out.

Late in the night Captain told Jesse, "It looks as if General Grant changed his strategy. Our cavalry detected his army shifting across the James River. They set up pontoon bridges to provide access. Columns filed across and marched toward Petersburg."

"Let's look at a map." Jesse took a frazzled map from his saddlebag. "Petersburg is only twenty-five miles south of Richmond but look at the railroads intersecting. The Richmond and Petersburg runs north and south; the Weldon, below Petersburg gives access to North Carolina and points south; the Norfolk leads to the Atlantic Ocean; the Richmond and Danville joins the Weldon at Richmond and moves our supplies west, and City Point moves material east to the James and Appomattox Rivers. I see why General Grant wants to control these railroads."

"Our essential war materials move over these rails. Constantly." Captain studied the map; then folded it for Jesse.

MONDAY/13. Jesse said, "We've spotted some Yanks. I think they are retreating. General Wade Hampton and his cavalry are following them.

"I wonder if this transfer of the Union Army caught General Lee by surprise. They can almost outflank our Rebel Army from Richmond." Captain unfolded his map.

"One of the boys found a copy of Harper's paper. It said that Union General Butler made a costly mistake. His Army of the James was at Fort Monroe over here, close to Newport News. They moved westward while General Grant moved the Army of the Potomac into the Wilderness.

"Our General Beauregard who was at Petersburg assembled 3,500 soldiers, militia, and shopkeepers. General Butler looked at that mass of men and lost his nerve. Look at Bermuda Hundred. The whole Army of the James withdrew there, placing themselves in this narrow gap.

"The paper reported that General Grant said, disgustedly, 'Butler's force is as completely shut off from further operations as if it had been in a bottle strongly corked.'"

"Mistakes lose battles. Correct cavalry information is vital to General Lee's decisions." Major closed his saddlebag.

TUESDAY/14. Jesse walked from his tent. "Captain, I'm sick as a dog. I've heaved my innards inside out."

"We don't have time for you to be sick. Go and see the medic."

"You've got a high, high fever. Infection somewhere. Are you cut anywhere?" The medic poured castor oil. "A Doctor Crawford has an office about eight miles down that road. Do you feel like riding that far?"

"You keep the castor oil. I'll find the doctor."

Doctor Crawford examined Jesse. "I've got a bed you can use. We'll take care of your horse. You're a sick young man."

THURSDAY/16. Doctor Crawford sat in a rickety oak chair, placed by Jesse's bed. With his right hand the doctor opened Jesse's eye. "Look down; then up; then to each side. Your fever's gone down some. Take this medicine after each meal and sleep as much as you can. I think you'll be able to go back to your duties tomorrow."

FRIDAY/17. Jesse saddled his horse and rode for camps. He saw an elderly couple, swinging on their front porch. "May I have a glass of water?"

"We're the Reynolds. Mother is waiting for her cornbread to finish baking. If you have time we'd like to serve you dinner. I'll get a glass of water for you."

Y'all are mighty kind to offer. I've got to get back to my unit. Your Doctor Crawford cured me from ailing. I always seem to have time for a home-cooked meal."

SATURDAY/18. Jesse rode to his camps located three miles from Richmond.

WITH DEAD LINES

SUNDAY/19. Jesse walked with Captain to the chaplain's tent. Jesse said, "I'm twenty-three year's old today. Reckon where we'll be this time next year if we're still alive?"

"Take one day at a time. We'll eat a Sunday Dinner in camps and spend the afternoon relaxing." Captain sat on a bench.

Jesse wrote home, "I haven't been there lately, but I hear that from the Potomac River to Petersburg lays one vast scene of desolation. Villages and farms are deserted and in ruins. Plows stand idle in uncultivated fields. Village blacksmith and carpenters' shops are gone. In one flour mill, though burned and smoking, its machinery continues in motion. If ever a country suffered the horrors of war it is Virginia."

WEDNESDAY/22. Captain said, "You know, Jesse, since the Confederacy decided that our cavalrymen must provide our own horses we may lose some good men. If they can't find horses for sale at prices they can afford they'll be forced into foot soldiers."

Jesse said, "Today, I can ride out into the surrounding country and recruit horses. I'm sure our people will support the war effort. I'll find the horses; then those boys who need them will have to come up with the money."

THURSDAY/23. The cavalry moved up the James River. Company C camped twenty miles from Richmond.

SATURDAY/25. They moved four miles farther up-river and camped in sight of Secretary Seddon's dwelling. Jesse said, "Captain, I don't like to be with the dead lines. This is my first time since the war commenced."

With nothing to do but sit around camp all day!

"Yeah. This war is getting to be a desperate affair. A man is not allowed to talk, yea, wink too loud." Captain rubbed oil into his saddle.

WEDNESDAY/29. Company C mounted up and rode three miles upriver to General Richard Anderson's place. They found very little forage for their horses.

THURSDAY/30. They rode up river and passed through Goochland. Captain stopped his horse in an open area. "We're about six miles above Goochland. Set up camps for the night."

JULY, 1864

FRIDAY/1. Jesse watched his horse munch grass. "The forage is much better here."

"It's very dry here but look at those thunderheads in the west, and feel the soft southern breeze. There's some prospect for rain soon."

Captain moistened his finger and held it up. "Yep, the breeze is straight out of the south."

"Today I'm reflecting upon my life as a soldier; this with pleasure but with great regret do I say that I am now with the dead line; first time since the war commenced. I told this to you a few days ago. It's really getting to me. The height of my ambition is to be on the frontier actively engaged. I enjoy better health and better pleasure." Jesse brushed his horse's mane.

"When we're idle we have too much time to think about what might be. Until the war is over, or we get killed, or wounded badly, we pretty well know that we'll fight more. I spend a lot of time thinking and planning—what if. What if the enemy catches me without my weapon? What if my horse gets killed? And I make decisions about what I can best do." Captain sipped coffee.

MONDAY/4. Jesse rose from his soldier's bed very early and wrote a letter to his mother. Captain shouted, "Mount up. We're moving up-river three miles."

After setting up camps Jo and Jesse found a bait of dewberries for dinner. Jo said, "These are the best we've had in our shop."

Jesse wiped his lips. "I hope and pray that we may have better in our shops before 4, July, 1865. Though, if this war continues, I'll be thankful to do this good. How unthankful a being I am to have been spared this far. May I be able and worthy to give due thanks and may the just God see proper to guide me in the future, for without His aid we can do nothing."

WEDNESDAY/6. Company C rode from the horse infantry camps for the James River and camped forty-six miles above Richmond, near Cartersville. While Jesse and Captain walked across a field Jesse kicked a clod of dirt. "Due to dry weather their crops have suffered very bad."

THURSDAY/7. They passed through Powhatten Courthouse. On the edge of town four boys stopped under some shade trees to cool their horses. A small blonde boy carried a large basket. "My mother sent y'all a very good dinner."

"Tell your mother this dinner is very acceptable and we thank her deeply." Jesse placed the clean white cloth over empty plates. He smiled as he watched the boy labor up the front porch steps.

FRIDAY/8. Jesse was invited to have dinner with Mr. Wills.

SUNDAY/10. Company C arrived in camps. They passed the command three miles north of Stony Creek Station. Captain rode from headquarters and announced, "Ole Jube, excuse me, our General Jubal Early moved his forces down the valley and threatened Washington from the north. If I learn any more details I'll advise you. Set up camps here."

MONDAY/11. The company performed drills, attacking, defending, retreating in orderliness. At the close of daylight Jesse told Captain, "Our horses are faring well."

"We've got to feed them plenty of grain and exercise them daily. I can see too many ribs." Captain rubbed his hand across his horse's rib cage.

From 11 through 22, July, Company C lived in their Stony Creek Camps. They drilled once each day. Their exercise was very light and good. A plenty of rain kept them close to camps. They played poker and checkers, having a good time. Mail came to camps regularly and duty continued light.

FRIDAY/29. Company C mounted up and rode away from Stony Creek Camps. They set up near Reams Station.

BATTLE OF THE CRATER

SATURDAY/30. Cannonading was unusually heavy. Yanks charged Rebel lines time and time again. Rebels repulsed each attack successfully. Late that night Captain announced, "Up near Petersburg the enemy succeeded in blowing up part of our fortifications. The earth exploded beneath them. Some of our men were killed."

SUNDAY/31. Jesse mopped sweat from his brow. He penned a note in his journal, "A lovely Sabbath morning. All is calm and quiet. My mind naturally turns back to by-gone days, when youth's fleeting moments were crowded with never to be repeated joys. Everything seemed so big, and Christmases like an eternity apart."

Captain interrupted. "The Army of the Potomac and Army of Northern Virginia have met for combat ever since 1862. We've fought across Virginia, Maryland, and Pennsylvania. The Battle of the Crater, near Petersburg, may have broken the stalemate.

A coal miner's dream

"We've spent several weeks in camps, as have many others. The Yankee grapevine has been stout lately. There has been very little else to do except talk. Gossipy soldiers know a whole lot about few things. And our Rebels learned bits and pieces about a mine the Yanks were working on."

Jesse rolled up his sleeves. "Captain, this is a lovely Sabbath morning Everything is so calm and quiet."

AUGUST, 1864

MONDAY/1. Company C mounted up and rode approximately fifteen miles to the old camps near Stony Creek.

WEDNESDAY/3. They left and rode for a new camp near Freeman's Bridge.

THURSDAY/4. Jesse looked across the rolling hills. "This is a very good camping place."

"You're right." Captain poured a cup of coffee. "That 'Battle of the Crater,' as they call it over there at Petersburg, could have been a disaster for us."

"What do you mean?"

"Well. All summer both armies are deadlocked, entrenched face to face, in impregnable and elaborate works at Petersburg. We've all been waiting, sniping, and figuring.

"A Yankee's regiment's commanding officer, a Lieutenant Colonel Henry Pleasants heard one of his enlisted men say something like, 'We could blow that damned fort out of existence if we could run a mine shaft under it.'

"It just happened that the colonel is a mining engineer and most of his men are coal miners from the Upper Schylkill coal region. The idea caught on fire. It moved up through the commands and finally General Grant gave permission to use it.

With crude tools the colonel's men began digging the shaft on 25, June. By 27, July, 8,000 pounds of powder stood ready to be exploded.

"Gossipy enlisted men know something about everything. Secrets are almost impossible to keep. General Lee's Army learned a lot about the mine. In fact, between the lines and shots Rebels yelled, 'When are y'all "Yankee Nigger lovers gonna blow us up? Come on, now.'

"Generals Grant, Meade, and Burnside agreed to detonate the mine at 3:30 A.M., on 30, July. Thousands of Yankee soldiers assembled behind the mine's entrance. A newspaper said that they licked their dry lips and shifted the weight of their bodies as they withstood the suspense. Many believed Armageddon was at hand. Irish cursed their luck. Some crossed themselves, said their 'Hail Marys,' and 'Our Fathers,' as a hedge while the Protestants observed with their usual scorn.

"Three-thirty A.M. came and went. Nothing happened. By 4:15, Colonel Pleasants knew something was wrong because he lit the fuse at 3:15. Two volunteers crawled into the shaft and found the dead fuse at its first splicing. At 4:45 the earth erupted.

"An officer reported, 'It was a magnificent spectacle and as the mass of earth went into the air it carried men, guns, carriages, and limbers. It spread out like an immense cloud as it reached its altitude.'

"The Union lines were so close that the mass appeared as if it would descend upon the waiting troops ready to charge. They broke and scattered to the rear. It took about ten minutes to reform and attack.

"Yankee artillery released a hammering salvo from 144 pieces. Smoke from the guns drifted forward and mixed with dust from the explosion. The rising sun became blood-red through the orange haze.

"The mine's explosion formed an irregular, elliptically shaped crater, 300 feet deep, about 60 feet wide, and over 170 feet long. When the Yankees approached the Crater everything fell apart for them. They became a disorganized crowd of spectators. They slid, and walked, and climbed all over it.

"Guts lay overturned. Broken gun carriages covered the ground. Military and fortification material was silent. Half buried Rebels moaned, some with only their heads and arms sticking out of the ground. Corpse's eyes stared, every bone in their bodies broken by the concussion. They found one Southern boy with both legs blown off, helplessly trying to crawl to safety, all the while, leaving two wakes of blood behind him from his dragging stumps. They saw an arm still holding a musket in its hand, the rope sling of which was intertwined through its lifeless fingers.

"The shock of the explosion wore off and Rebels took advantage of Yankee confusion. Small arms and field pieces loaded with grapeshot, canister, and any scrap that would fit down the muzzles poured murderous fire into soldiers packed in the Crater. Unparalleled horror lived in it. In places panic-stricken Yankees packed together. They couldn't move, not even raise an arm to defend themselves. Dead and wounded couldn't fall to the ground. Blood, brains, bone fragments spattered the living men. Often those who were able to fall were stomped beyond recognition by boots and shoes of their terror stricken comrades. Many wounded were trampled to death.

"Rebels' close-range gunfire gouged. Artillery shrapnel crashed. Mortar shells exploded into lethal fragments, smashing the Blue to scraps, tearing off heads, and arms; ripping bodies to bloody pulp. Furious, spitting, cursing yelling Rebels continued to move in and destroy Yankees with unabated vengeance.

"Our men ran out of ammunition. Some of them fixed bayonets on their rifles and threw them for spears, harpooning the Yanks. Others threw rocks bottles, anything dangerous. From the close range fighting blood ran down in streams in the hard brown clay and formed pools in which men slipped and it got on everything.

"By 10:30, with the sun higher, the Yankees suffered dreadfully. Hot thirsty, and out of ammunition, some of them tried to get back to their trenches but that hundred yards was raked by our deadly crossfire.

"We whipped them severely. Sometimes the dead and dying were piled eight deep. General Saunders' Alabama Brigade arrived to shore up our troops. They crept to the Crater's edge, put their caps and hats on ramrods and raised them.

"It fooled the Yankee troops and those who could, fired a volley. The Alabama boys charged into the hole before the Yanks could reload and a furious hand-to-hand battle began. With rifle butts men bashed each others brains out and stabbed one another to death with bayonets. Fist fights broke out. Soldiers groveled among the dead and wounded in the blood and dust.

"Surviving Yanks surrendered by the hundreds. Scared ones fled to safety by the thousands. Their retreat became a rout. Rebels chased them through thick battle smoke. They suffered bedlam. Some who were shot at such close range had powder burns on their bodies.

"Yanks' cannons remained silent. We massacred them this time."

Jesse said, "I wish we'd been there."

"There were 4,000 Federal casualties. We suffered 1,200." Captain walked away.

FIGHT FOR PETERSBURG

MONDAY/8. Jesse rode with a foraging party, searching along the Blackwater River which flowed east and south of Petersburg.

"Hot dog. Look at all those green apples." A rider pointed.

"We might get belly aches from apples but I see a field full of watermelons. I'll just thump one or two and find out if they're ripe." Jesse stopped his horse.

Captain said, "Before y'all take anything, there's a farmer, loading his gun—over yonder by the barn."

Jesse led his horse to the man. "Good morning, Sir. Our camps are a few miles up the river and food is running out. Can we buy some of your apples and watermelons?"

"Young man, it's a good thing you took time to ask. Keep your eye on that jug of water hanging yonder." Gently a breeze moved the jug back and forth. The old man cocked his gun, aimed; fire. "Where did it go?"

"The same place I'd gone if I didn't ask." Jesse laughed. "What will you take for twenty bushels of apples and a hundred melons?"

"I've got some bushel baskets right here in the barn. For every two bushels you pick I'll give you one. And for every melon you load in the wagon you can put one in the other wagon. If you can wait until tomorrow to go back to camps I'll haul the stuff for you."

"If you promise to put your gun in a closet we'll do anything to help you."

TUESDAY/9. Slick, shiny mules strained at the wagon in the early morning.

WEDNESDAY/10. After a drenching rain the weather turned pleasant Jesse said, "I hear cannonading up toward Petersburg."

"I believe." Captain chose his words carefully. "I believe General Grant has realized that his siege tactics—a series of regular drives by which his heavy artillery got close enough to flatten our fortifications didn't succeed against the earthern works."

"Well. He's kept General Lee frustrated and under pressure with all those surprise attacks north of the James River and on Richmond's front." Jesse unfolded his tattered map.

Captain placed his finger on Petersburg. "At the same time General Grant extended his left line to the west and north, forcing us to stretch our thinly held line. If Grant can encircle Petersburg he will block all vital roads and railroads. He might starve us into surrender or force us to abandon Richmond and move south."

THURSDAY/11. Company C rode from camps near Sussex Courthouse. Jesse said, "Rumors are that we're to go to the Valley."

"Our orders are to camp five miles from Petersburg." Captain spurred his horse.

FRIDAY/12. At daybreak the bugler sounded Reveille. Company C rode through Petersburg and camped five miles south of Richmond. All riders whose horses were unshod stopped with the blacksmiths.

SATURDAY/13. Columns formed and rode north to Ashland. While blacksmiths' hammers gonged on anvils, shaping horseshoes. Captain's voice sounded, "Mount up."

"It's much against our wishes but we are ordered to New Market twelve miles south of Richmond."

Company C rode into breastworks at 11:00 P.M.

MONDAY/15. They remained in breastworks during the day; then moved out at nightfall.

TUESDAY/16. They commenced building their own works at midnight and finished at daylight.

The Rebel brigade on the Charles City Road went to their left, scouting Union Generals Gregg and Gary's infantry. Rebels engaged the enemy at approximately 8:00 A.M. Yankee infantry, cavalry, and artillery formed a large force. Yelling Rebels charged and drove the Yankees quite handsomely for three quarters of a mile. But the Yankees moved behind the Rebels' breastworks and forced them to fall back.

Jesse's eyes winced. "A minnie ball hit my left leg. It's a slight wound."

Soon with reinforcements, the Rebels drove the Yankees for one mile, capturing large numbers of prisoners and horses. Company C returned to their breastworks and threw up more.

Jesse told Captain, "I'm very tired."

"Get that wound dressed. Some medics are with the wagons."

WEDNESDAY/17. Jesse remained in the breastworks.

"Captain, I'm mighty hungry but what bothers me more than that is being separated from our horses."

"I can't help your hunger; however, you'll be happy to know that we'll be relieved at noon and can return to our horses." Captain placed a rifle against a log.

THURSDAY/18. Company C traveled the Williamsburg Road and found their brigade near Savage's Station.

SUNDAY/21. They left Oak Swamp for the right side of their lines below Petersburg. When they arrived at the James River they rode across on a pontoon bridge. Jesse remarked, "This is my first experience with such a crossing."

Captain said, "General Lee wired Richmond that our supply of corn is exhausted and our small reserve is consumed. Starvation is now a strong possibility."

MONDAY/22. Company C rode through Petersburg and camped eight miles south of said place. Because their horses got no forage they began to break down very fast.

WEDNESDAY/24. Jesse rode picket two miles from Reams Station. After being relieved he rode to camps eight miles west from said place.

THURSDAY/25. At 3:00 A.M. he was in the saddle again, attacking Yankees and driving them three miles to their breastworks. The line of which Jesse was a member joined General A. P. Hill at 3:00 P.M. They made one grand and glorious charge.

General Wade Hampton, commander of the Confederate Cavalry Corps, sent word to General Lee that the Union V Corps had seized the Weldon Railroad at Globe Tavern. Rains made roads nearly impassable south of the Appomattox River. By the evening of 24, August, the infantry of the Union's II Corps had ripped up the track to a point three miles south of Reams Station. Union General Hancock's force consisted of about 6,000 infantry, 2,000 cavalry, and 16 guns.

General Hampton asked General Lee to send infantry to join the cavalry in an attack on Hancock's forces. Lee sent eight brigades of infantry under General A. P. Hill. The whole Rebel force consisted of about 5,000 infantry, 5,000 cavalry, and 20 guns. "In order to avoid the Yankees at Globe Tavern General Hill led his Rebels in a circling, night movement on 24, August Heading south, General Hill used the Squirrel Level Road. When they reached a safe distance beyond Globe Tavern, they switched over to the Vaughn Road which moved more easterly. Those men spent the night at Armstrong's Mill The Vaughn Road crossed a tributary of Rowanty Creek, Hatcher's Run.

On the morning of 25, August, General Hill continued south of the Vaughn Road to Monk's Neck Road. His troops moved east on Monk's Neck Road. They crossed Rowanty Creek and Stopped at the edge of Reams Station.

General Hampton began the battle at 8:00 A.M. Cavalry broke through Union General Gregg's picket line which ran from Reams Station east to the Jerusalem Plank Road. Heavy skirmishing developed near the railroad. Hampton's cavalry occupied the works and Rebel infantry returned to the nearly empty trenches at Petersburg.

Rebels killed and wounded 610 Yankees, took at least 1752 prisoners, took 12 colors, 9 guns, and 3100 stands of arms.

Yankees killed and wounded 720 Rebels.

Even with the Reams Station victory General Lee couldn't use the Weldon Railroad any farther north than Stony Creek Depot, sixteen miles south of Petersburg. There the Rebels loaded supplies into wagons for a cross-country journey to Dinwiddie Court House, by way of Flat Foot Road. From Dinwiddie, Rebel wagons trudged Boydton Plank Road into Petersburg.

FRIDAY/26. Company C returned to the camps.

SATURDAY/27. Jesse left camps to ride picket near Reams Station.

SUNDAY/28. He returned to camps. "Captain, it's good to get plenty to eat."

"Our food supply is seriously threatened."

WEDNESDAY/31. Jesse said, "Every now and then I enjoy these kinds of quiet and calm days. Today I received three sausages from my sister. Good sausages make me think of home."

"You are probably thinking about Sallie Belle and wondering how much she has grown." Captain smiled.

"By now, she's fourteen; going on fifteen. I'm sure she is beginning to look as if she is a young lady and no longer a little girl. Her writing has matured." Jesse reached into his shirt pocket and removed Madge, now a dirty, blood-stained doll.

SEPTEMBER, 1864

THURSDAY/1. Jesse rode picket. He had a quiet time.

FRIDAY/2. After midnight some sentries fired on Yankee scouts who passed through the lines.

At daybreak Yanks attacked and drove the Rebel pickets. Jesse rode forward with Company C to retake their post. He fired at and chased off a Yankee cavalryman; then rode on to his post. There he found Yankee infantry. They fired at him.

After Rebels re-established their lines at 10:00 A.M., Company C was relieved and returned to camps.

SATURDAY/3. Jesse's horse foundered.

SUNDAY/4. Camps remained quiet.

MONDAY/5. Jesse rode into the country and using his knife, cut some vegetables from a farmer's fall garden. He smiled while smoke circled from his small fire, and water bubbled around some potatoes. "Nothing beats home cooking."

TUESDAY/6. Jesse awakened early. "I hear heavy firing toward Petersburg."

Captain said, "I'm sure General Grant intends doing something."

WEDNESDAY/7. While marching guard duty Jesse told Captain, "I feel uncommonly good."

"I'm glad somebody can feel good. There are no signs of peace."

"I didn't say that I feel good about the war." Jesse bit into some tobacco. "General Hood and the Army of Tennessee evacuated Atlanta on the first. Think about all the ammunition and stores they destroyed simply because they weren't able to carry them away. Yankee troops on the city's outskirts reported seeing billows of smoke and fire in the night air and feeling shock waves reverberating."

Captain added, "Hardee withdrew his men and rendezvoused with our army, leaving Atlanta."

"I heard about General Richard Anderson's Corps which General Early sent toward Richmond. At Berryville Anderson ran into part of General Sherman's Army. After a hard fight the Rebels retreated to Winchester to our main body of troops."

Captain frowned. "While we're talking about General 'Jube,' I think his troops continue to clash with the Yanks along the Opequon Creek."

"We'll stay in camps."

FRIDAY/9. Company C rode in line from their camps. At 3:00 P.M. on McDonald's Farm they met the enemy. A sharp skirmish commenced. Soon it turned into a regular battle. Rebels charged, over-ran, and captured the Yanks' breastworks. Company C rounded up many prisoners. Jesse captured a fine horse equipped with a new bridle and saddle.

Supremely, quietness ruled over camps.

MONDAY/19. Dempsey and John strolled towards Jesse's tent. He ran to meet them. "Am I seeing ghosts or what?"

"Or what." John smiled. "I brought a package from Mrs. Sparkman."

Jesse opened his knife and cut the strings. He unfolded two pairs of hand-knitted boot socks. He placed a new linen handkerchief over his nose and snorted. He held ear-muffs over each ear. "Did you boys say something? Y'all brought some good clothes from Mother. Thanks. I'll write to her and when you go back home I'll appreciate your carrying the letter to her. We don't know how much of our mail goes through."

Dempsey said, "Henry, I've brought a package to you from the children."

Henry looked into his package and closed it quickly. "Y'all don't want to see what they sent."

"I showed what Mother sent. Let's see yours."

Henry re-opened his package but held it at a safe distance from the others. "Here are some butter cookies, some ginger-bread, some chocolate cake, and taffy. Surely you don't want any."

"What a joyful evening we'll have. We can take you boys to see some of your ol' friends here in camps, and play cards until y'all have to be out. And we'll eat Henry's goodies." Jesse placed his package on his saddle-bags.

Captain said, "I heard about a rather humiliating event for the Yanks. General Wade Hampton led a daring raid of 4,000 Rebel horsemen around the Army of the Potomac and returned with more than 2,400 head of cattle and 300 prisoners."

"I think it was a bold and clever trick. We deserve every head after such a raid." Jesse packed tobacco into his corncob pipe. "Rebels saw the cattle grazing in some high grass opposite Harrison's Landing on the Blackwater. General Gregg sent Yankee cavalry with the 2nd Division to pursue our boys but they re-crossed the river safely."

Captain said, "This was a desperate attempt to alleviate the Army of North Virginia's hunger. It can't last. General Grant will continue tightening his noose around us."

THURSDAY/29. Quietly in pre-dawn darkness General Grant slipped General Birney's X Corps and General Ord's XVIII Corps back across the James River in a surprise move against Richmond's outer defenses.

Jesse said, "My guess is General Grant did that primarily to prevent General Lee's re-enforcing General Jube in the Shenandoah Valley. It might force General Lee to weaken part of our Petersburg line."

Captain said, "We received word that General Birney was repulsed a mile and a half above Fort Harrison on the Varina Road. That would be an attack on Fort Gilmer on the New Market Road."

"General Ord stormed Fort Harrison."

FRIDAY/30. General Lee with re-enforcements, including Generals Archibald Gracie and Hoke's divisions, and four of General George Pickett's regiments, directed several vigorous assaults against Fort Harrison. Lee's men found the rear of the Yankees' works closed-in and strengthened. Under fire from new, repeating rifles, the Rebels fell back, suffering heavy losses.

Again General Meade sent reconnaissance forces to the west.

General Hampton's cavalry and Johnson's division of infantry stopped them at Peeble's Farm. General Meade extended his left flank another three miles west of the Weldon Railroad forcing General Lee to stretch his defensive line. Now with fewer than 50,000 troops he held a 35-mile line from north of Richmond to west of Petersburg.

Jesse rode picket at Moss Creek Bridge. Company C experienced heavy skirmishing on the Farley Lines.

OCTOBER, 1864

THURSDAY/6. Jesse rotated on and off picket, camping near the grapevine.

General Lee sent word to President Davis, "The enemy's position enables him to move his troops to the right or left without our knowledge until he has reached the point at which he aims and we are then compelled to hurry our men to meet him, incurring the risk of being too late to check his progress and the additional risk of the advantage he may derive from their absence.

"Without some increase of strength, I cannot see how we can escape the natural consequences of the enemy's numerical superiority. If things thus continue, the most serious consequences must result."

FRIDAY/7. Yanks advanced and drove-in Rebel pickets.

SATURDAY/8. At daybreak a fight commenced and lasted all day. Company C fell back to the Boydton Plank Road. A general engagement erupted. Severely, Rebels punished Yanks for their bold demonstration. Yanks fell back during the night leaving their dead and wounded on the field.

Weather turned cloudy; then cold. Snow began falling. Jesse tightened his collar. "This duty is uncommonly hard."

Captain said, "As surely as summer followed spring, winter will follow this fall. This may well be our worst times."

SATURDAY/ 15. In early morning heavy frost covered camps. Boys hammered and nailed, building crude huts to be lived in for winter quarters.

"All right, Boys. Let's take a break from work. Some of you have been discussing who owns the fastest horse in Company C. We've got a good half-mile track around the drill field. We'll run six horses at a time and those winners will run against each other to determine our fastest horse."

Contestants lined up. Boys bet among themselves. Jesse fired his pistol. Horses plunged from the line. Riders talked to and whipped their horses. Spectators cheered their chosen winners. Jesse announced winners and money changed hands.

OH SHENANDOAH

A spectacular sun rose above the nearly completed winter quarters on 14, October. Captain said, "When we finish our quarters, we've yet to build stables."

"Our boys are quite over-joyed about blissful imaginings of the future." Jesse spit on a hammer.

Captain said, "Anticipation of going South rages high. I have a beautiful mental picture. I recall plowing with our gray mare. Tender green leaves covered the trees. Busy birds carried straw in their beaks for their nests and freshly plowed earth smelled sweet. I hope to find the reality of those memories soon."

Jesse smiled.

SUNDAY/16. "A lovely Sabbath. The war is over for me." Japtha packed his saddle bags. He mounted his horse and started a long journey home.

Throughout camp men relaxed, washed clothes, and cleaned weapons. Jesse told Captain, "There's very little hay and no corn for our horses."

While Company C of the Jeff Davis Legion, Mississippi Cavalry, worked on winter quarters, General Jubal Early led his Rebels in a surprise attack at Cedar Creek, near Strasburg. In panic Yanks fled.

Union General Sheridan rode from Winchester, rallied the Yanks and counterassaulted, routing the Rebels. Now Sheridan controlled the Shenandoah.

"You know, Jesse, the Shenandoah Valley was mighty important to us for food and forage. Here we are in mid-October. Our Confederate manpower has dwindled from massive casualties suffered during many victories."

Jesse sewed a patch on the knee of his pants. "And General Grant continues strengthening the Federal Army with more and more available men. They are equipped with new repeating rifles. Food and supplies move to them on waterways and railroads. Our Confederate generals are the best in the land.

They know war skills and have excellent rapport but our manpower pool is running dry."

Captain frowned. "General Grant ain't giving any rest to our half-starved, weary Rebels.

"On Thursday, Grant detached Generals Hancock and Warren to the Boydton Plank Road. Cavalry screened them.

"General Hampton's Cavalry, with Generals Heth and Mahone struck Hancock at Burgess' Mill right there where the road crosses Hatcher's Run. Rebels forced the Yanks to withdraw. Needless to say, Rebels remain in control of Boydton Plank Road."

FRIDAY/28. Company C moved forward to reestablish their former picket lines. They returned to camps near General Young's Headquarters.

NOVEMBER, 1864

TUESDAY/1. Company C packed-up and moved camps to Wilson's Farm close to Boydton Plank Road.

WEDNESDAY/2. Jesse found the 11th Mississippi Regiment. They worked on their winter quarters. Jesse strolled to the foot of a ladder, which was propped against a crude hut. "I'm from the Mississippi Cavalry and we've been working on some winter quarters, too. I reckon bad weather is coming soon."

A soldier replied, "I sort of dread settling into an awful monotony of living here through the cold winter."

"Find a hammer for me and I'll help you drive nails. I've got the day off from Company C." Jesse grabbed a hammer.

"Where in Mississippi do you hail from?"

"Cooksville."

"Never heard of it."

After the sun dropped beneath the horizon Jesse said, "I've enjoyed a pleasant day with you boys."

SUNDAY/6. The sun rose into a clear sky. Ice covered shallow ditches. Water buckets froze solid. Boys huddled around small fires and held their hands over flames. One said, "You know, I don't mind this cold weather while I'm anticipating going South."

"What makes your courage tolerable plentiful is a belly full of good rations." Jesse rubbed his hands together.

"And our horses are doing finely." Another boy held a bucket full of mixed feed.

"On the whole we're doing as well as soldiers can expect." Jesse warmed his gloves.

SUNDAY/13. At breakfast Captain told Jesse, "Well. Soon we will leave for Stony Creek."

"I thought we were going South."

Captain smiled. "We're going South all right. South of Petersburg. We regret leaving our winter quarters."

"I declare. We've worked together without intermission for twenty-eight days and now we're leaving before we benefit from our labor." Jesse packed his saddlebags.

"War isn't concerned about our feelings." Captain examined his bridle.

"May time hurry in her flight and flee over our present struggle."

WEDNESDAY/30. Early in the morning Captain's voice rang out, "Fall in and be prepared to meet the enemy on Vaughn Road."

Company C formed a strong line near the road and waited until dark. No Yanks came.

DECEMBER, 1864

THURSDAY/1. Yanks attacked and captured Stony Creek with a garrison of 125 men. Company C rode from camps on Wilson's Farm for assistance. They arrived at Stony Creek too late. Yanks captured five of Company C's boys.

SATURDAY/3. Camps moved from Wilson's Farm to within three miles of Stony Creek Depot.

WEDNESDAY/7. Company C rode from camps to meet the enemy. After riding all night Rebels collided with Yanks near Garrett's Station. Skirmishing followed. General Wade Hampton outflanked the Yanks and the right flank headed them to Bill's Field. Company C camped near the Double Bridges.

FRIDAY/9. Cold weather cut through Jesse's tattered uniform. Many boys burned fences freely. Their fires' warm glow attracted first their front sides; then their backs.

Company C rode from camps at 3:00 A.M. and galloped onto Bill's Field at 9:00 A.M. Skirmishing commenced.

SATURDAY/10. Yanks fell back during the morning. Weather turned very cold. Sleet began to cover the ground. In their retreat Yanks set fire to barns, dwellings, buildings of any sort, and fodder stacks in the fields.

SUNDAY/11. Company C reached camps. Jesse said, "When I was growing up, Sundays were always special. Church and family came first. We've been riding horses all day."

"The Confederacy is supreme now. I hate to think about what will become of the South if we lose our fight." Captain walked towards Headquarters.

THURSDAY/15. One of the boys said to Jesse, "I heard by the grapevine that we're moving camps again."

"I don't know. When I think we have a permanent camp for winter quarters we are called to ride." Jesse bit into a juicy apple.

"All right. Company C, Mount up in fifteen minutes." Captain buttoned his coat and put on his gloves.

Company C rode from camps near Stony Creek Depot. "Look out Ballsville. Here we come." Jesse smiled.

SUNDAY/18. At 4:00 P.M. the company rode into camps located one mile out of Ballsville.

MONDAY/19. Early in the morning camps buzzed. Soldiers carried hewn logs, pegs, hammers, hatchets, and cypress shingles. Winter quarters inched into shape. Jesse looked over the activity. "I am very much pleased with camps."

TUESDAY/20. Jesse walked from the Quartermaster holding a bottle. "I don't know about you, Captain, but this is a memorable day for me. It's the first since the war commenced for me to draw brandy. I think I'll give it to the sick."

"Oh. I'm developing a terrible headache. I need something to help me relax." Captain placed his head in his hands and peeked through his fingers.

Jesse handed the brandy to him.

WEDNESDAY/21. The weather became very rainy and disagreeable.

SUNDAY/25. After a Christmas Dinner of baked turkey and sweet potatoes boys stood near small fires warming themselves. A good quantity of brandy passed from hand to hand and from fire to fire. Some boys began to sing Christmas hymns and practice the Rebel Yell. Others began to laugh and stagger from campfire to campfire shouting, "Merry Christmas. Merry Christmas."

JANUARY, 1865

SUNDAY/1. "It's a New Year's Day and I'm having a fine time in camp. I've got a genuine leather folding stool. The dirt in my winter quarters is dry. There aren't any rats, most likely because there isn't any food left over for them." Jesse sat upon his stool.

"I've been inspecting some of the troops. It's interesting to watch enthusiasm generated by boys who are excited about furloughs." Captain sat on the floor.

There are hardly any railroad cars in this vicinity. The boys will have a hard time going South." Jesse whittled on a piece of cedar.

WEDNESDAY/4. Captain saluted Jesse. "On this beautiful winter morning you have just been promoted to acting Major. Congratulations.

Walk up to Headquarters with me and I'll review the details with you. I'm going South."

Strolling from Headquarters Jesse frowned. "The details are quite numerous and the duty uncommonly hard."

"You can handle them. I believe in you."

TUESDAY/10. Rain commenced falling in torrents. Jesse put on a worn out rain cape and trudged in ankle-deep mud to General Headquarters. He overheard a staff officer say, "I don't see how the coming spring can bring much hope to General Lee's Army. His men are starving and freezing in filthy trenches."

Another continued. "And desertion and disease are slowly eroding his once proud Army of Northern Virginia. I heard from a pretty good source that more than 2900 slipped off into the darkness to go home and not return."

Jesse said, "Recruiting and drafting can't keep pace with his losses. MY gut feeling is, Company C's boys are excited and their spirits are high as they anticipate furloughs. I believe they'll all come back."

"How do you like acting a major's role?" One asked.

"My duty proves to be a good way to pass time in camps."

SUNDAY/15. Jesse and several boys watched smoke curl from a small fire. One of them said, "Here we are in winter quarters on a Sunday, passing off time quite pleasantly."

"It's pleasant weather. Looks like spring." Another added.

Jesse said, "I feel very lonesome and wish I could spend the day at home."

AND NOW—SOUTH CAROLINA

TUESDAY/17. Jesse passed the word, "Boys, we are ordered to go to South Carolina."

"South Carolina?" A voice trailed away.

"Yes." Jesse frowned. "Anticipation of horse details are gone through unmitigated shades."

WEDNESDAY/18. Jesse ordered, "Company C, Mount up."

Their march commenced. They stayed all night at Colliers' Farm.

THURSDAY/19. At daybreak Jesse saddled his horse. Company C rode all day and camped at Gaston, North Carolina.

FRIDAY/20. They crossed the Roanoke River and rode into the car camps nearby.

SATURDAY/21. Jesse listened to tree limbs crack. At daybreak he heard a voice shout, "Wake up everybody. It's very unpleasant weather. It's sleeting."

SUNDAY/22. They rode with care.

MONDAY/23. They camped near Henderson, North Carolina. Jesse told his boys, "Build small fires close together and stand between them. It's very cold and we don't want any frost-bite."

TUESDAY/24. They camped on the Tar River.

WEDNESDAY/25. They camped near Stagville.

THURSDAY/26. They camped near Hillsborough.

FRIDAY/27. They camped near Graham's Depot.

Jesse's spurs clanged as he strolled along a board walk to a general store. Its door creaked when he pulled it and a red-hot, pot-bellied stove provided warmth to his hands. A lady smiled. "May I help you, Sir?"

"Excuse me for staring at you Mam." Jesse blushed. He held Madge and smiled. "A little girl in Mississippi gave this rag-doll to me and it saved my life, by stopping a minnie-ball, headed for my heart. And you are the second lady who reminds me of the little girl. I'm Lieutenant Sparkman."

"My name is Annie Kirkpatrick. And I'm tending the store while my father is out cutting wood."

"He's going to have to cut a lot of wood if y'all keep that stove red-hot." Jesse rubbed his hands together.

"Will you be in town very long? Many soldiers have been passing through." Her eyes met his.

"I came into your store to find out if you have any coffee I can buy. Like the others, I'm just passing through." Jesse weaved his hand into tangled hair and replaced his cap.

"The store doesn't have any coffee but we have some tea at our home. It's a few blocks that way. Mother will fix supper for you?" Annie waited for a reply.

"We're going to camp here. And I don't have duty tonight. I'd be happy to join y'all."

After Jesse rode into camps, three of his boys sat near a fire. One said, "Lieutenant, you're mighty late, considering we've got to ride early in the morning."

"A bouncing lass invited me to supper and we enjoyed the evening. And besides, Company C won't move until afternoon. Miss Moria Montgomery, Miss Annie's friend invited me to dinner."

"And we're eatin' hard tack."

SATURDAY/28. After dinner Jesse galloped fifteen miles in two hours and rode into camps. "All right, Boys, Let's go. Mount up."

SUNDAY/ 29. Company C found camps of Greensboro. One of the boys pointed. "There's a big house on fire."

Jesse and several riders galloped to the front yard, where a group of people huddled in the morning's coldness. A lady wiped tears from her eyes. "Three of my neighbors are burning to death in their house and it's too far gone for anyone to stop it."

"I'm sorry, Mam. We have enough men to form a bucket brigade but that won't help." Jesse placed his cap over his heart.

They moved camps four miles west of Greensboro. After blacksmiths shod their horses Company C ate supper and bedded down.

MONDAY/30. They rode hard all day.

TUESDAY/31. They camped near Thomastown.

FEBRUARY, 1865

WEDNESDAY/1. Jesse commanded, "Company C, Fall in. This is a beautiful day, Boys. The country is somewhat better than usual. We'll take it easy today and camp on the Yadkin River banks tonight."

THURSDAY/2. They passed through Salisburg and camped near China Grove. Jesse said, "Rebels are holding quite a number of prisoners in Salisburg."

"How are we feeding them?" A boy smiled.

"Very little." Jesse said.

FRIDAY/3. Company C camped seven miles from Concord.

SATURDAY/4. Riding through Charlotte Jesse nodded his head to the right. "There are some pretty women on the streets."

Thirteen miles from Catawba River Company C camped. "Look. I see a great many wild geese."

Their horses were well down.

THURSDAY/9. The company reached camps on Pees Farm near Catawba River, in Fairfield District, South Carolina.

TUESDAY/14. On foot they left Pees Farm for Ridgeway Depot. "This is quite a fatiguing march. Boys, we'll mount the cars at 5:00 P.M. for Columbia, South Carolina."

WEDNESDAY/15. They passed through Columbia and reached camps. Jesse said, "We'll eat a snack; then march to the front."

That night, they evacuated their lines and fell back to Columbia and camped on city streets.

General Sherman and his 60,000 battle-hardened Yankees abandoned their supply lines and smashed into South Carolina. Yankees left Confederate coastal fortresses to be secured by Federal naval and amphibious forces. They captured Fort Fisher, which closed the last major access to the sea.

THURSDAY/16. Company C took position on the left of their lines. Yankees shelled Columbia, killing some non-combatants. At nightfall Company C marched back to the State House, got their horses, and drew ordnance.

Mounted on his horse, Jesse stopped on a small knoll at the city limits. His eyes walked along a wide, dirt street. Directly in front of him lay parts of what once had been a sturdy, plank fence. His eyes darted from burned out building to burned out building. Brick wall sections and tall chimneys stood helplessly in the glow.

Personal belongings and furnishings of buildings glimmered in various hues. Trees with their branches charred reached out, groping for cool fresh air. In the fire and smoke's immense heat floated burning paper and cloth, landing over the city. A signpost which once carried the street name proudly, smoldered, a mere stump.

Jesse told Al Anthony, "I'll not try to picture this awful destruction but future historians may dwell upon tonight's results with tears in their eyes."

"The city must surrender." Al wiped sweat from his forehead.

FRIDAY/17. General Sherman's Army marched into Columbia. The city surrendered at 10:00 A.M. Along-side many Rebels, Jesse marched out and camped ten miles away. Words circulated from Rebel to Rebel, "Charleston surrendered to the U. S. Navy today, also."

SATURDAY/18. Company C skirmished. They camped near Duca Depot.

SUNDAY/19. While Jesse rode picket, Yankees charged his post. Only two men rode with him. "I'm quite willing to give plenty of distance between us."

"Yeah. Let's skedaddle." Al spurred his horse.

They rode fourteen miles after dark and camped at Winnsboro.

MONDAY/20. Company C marched through Winnsboro and camped nine miles north of said place.

WEDNESDAY/22. They left camps for the Yanks' right flank. When night fell Company C occupied a high position. Jesse watched many houses go up in flames. He camped at Anderson's Mill on Fisher's Creek.

THURSDAY/23. Jesse told his men, "The enemy is pressing and we've got to cross the Catawba. It's a bad ford. Follow me."

FRIDAY/24. Jesse sent a message to Headquarters, "Company C is moving on the enemy's flank with great success."

SATURDAY/25. Near the Little Lynch River, Company C captured a number of prisoners and wagons. The Yanks wounded Al Anthony and captured McGraw. The company camped on the river bank.

SUNDAY/26. Jesse watched several Yankees carry sacks of stolen chickens and lead milk cows. "Pass the word for our company to mount up and circle those foragers. When I signal, everybody yell and force those boys to the river. Don't waste any ammunition on them."

Jesse held his hand high. Moved it forward. Rebels yelled. Horses snorted. Chickens cackled and fluttered in many directions. Cows moo-ed. Yankees jumped into the Lynch.

MONDAY/27. Company C remained in camps until 12:00 midnight. Jesse shouted, "Mount up, Boys. We are starting for Cheraw."

TUESDAY/28. After galloping their horses all night Company C slowed to a trot. Al said, "Times like this are very disagreeable on the men and hard on the horses."

"I know." Jesse patted his horse's neck. "The weather ought to be warming up in March."

By 4:00 P.M., the company rode into Cheraw.

MARCH, 1865

WEDNESDAY/1. Early in the morning Jesse yelled, "Mount up. We'll scout the area to ten miles south of Cheraw; then ride back into camps at almost dark."

At midnight, Jesse ordered, "Mount up. We're riding for Chesterfield, Chesterfield, South Carolina. Don't say it. I'll say it for you. The weather has become very cold, windy, and disagreeable. I can't do a thing about it."

THURSDAY/2. The company rode into Chesterfield. At 2:00 P.M. Yankees drove in the Rebel pickets. Skirmish commenced.

FRIDAY/3. Jesse rode among his boys. "Commence our retreat towards Cheraw."

As they rode within seven miles of said place a courier met them. "I've got orders that the enemy is about to cut us off. General Sherman's troops are in Cheraw. Change your retreat route."

Jesse stopped his horse at the edge of a running stream. "I'm going to set fire to the bridge because no other preparation has been made."

Company C watched the bridge go up in flames. A voice said, "That'll stop the Yanks for a while."

Three miles east of Cheraw the company set up camp. Some very patriotic ladies brought wagons loaded with home-cooked food and wine to the company. An elderly lady said, "There was a warehouse filled with great commissary stores but the Yankees destroyed them. Cheraw's ladies want to help the Rebel cause and we can feed soldiers now and then."

"Mam, you don't know how much we thank y'all for this kind act." Jesse removed his cap and bowed to the lady.

Nearly every soldier drank until they became salubrious.

"Your boys are over-doing themselves with the wine but they need some relaxation." She laughed. "Look at that boy, riding backwards on his horse. By-the-way, we were told that Union General Sheridan captured most of General Jubal Early's remnants at Waynesboro, Virginia, destroyed the Virginia Central Railroad, and is marching south to join General Grant at Petersburg."

"That's bad news but thanks for sharing it." Jesse sipped a glass of wine.

"Excuse me." Al walked away with Jesse. "There is speculation that General Lee must evacuate Petersburg and attempt moving south to join forces with General Joe Johnston and us here in the Carolinas."

Jesse said, "As General in Chief of the Confederate Forces General Lee reinstated General Johnston to Commander of the Army of Tennessee. General

Johnston moved into North Carolina from Mississippi, attempting to contain General Sherman. The Army of Tennessee is a pitiful shadow of a once proud Army. The fragmentary regiments total nearly 18,000 men."

SATURDAY/4. Jesse sat on his horse watching the enemy cross the Pee Dee River. Jesse ordered, "Charge." Men and horses skirmished. Company C set fire to their commissary stores and ordnance. Large explosions shook the earth. Flames reached for the sky.

Company C retreated to a position seven miles east of Cheraw and camped. Jesse told Al, "The cloud that is hovering around us is dark but for some unknown reason I am in good spirits. I have no doubts about our future."

SUNDAY/5. The company rode through some poor country. They arrived in Rockingham, North Carolina. People walked from stores and waved to the soldiers. Jesse smiled and said, "These are the ugliest women I ever saw."

"As long as they are women I don't complain." Al waved his cap to a young lady and she waved a kerchief."

"Some way, Sundays are rough for me. If I could see my ma and loved ones far away I would be happy." Jesse galloped his horse.

MONDAY/6. Company C remained in Rockingham all day; then camped nearby. At 12:00 midnight, Yanks ran Rebel pickets and continued their charge until they reached Company C's camp.

TUESDAY/7. A voice screamed, "Yanks driving in our pickets."

Jesse ordered, "Prepare to retire, skirmishing with the enemy. Re-enforcements from the Rebel Army of Tennessee arrived in Kingston, North Carolina, today."

Company C camped fourteen miles north of Rockingham, North Carolina.

WEDNESDAY/8. In the early morning Jesse ordered, "Company C. Mount up. We're riding for Fayetteville."

At 12:00 noon Company C met the enemy, charged, and drove them for two miles. Fourteen Yanks killed one good Rebel soldier.

The company retired six miles from the Petersburg & Goldsboro Railroad and camped.

General Wade Hampton spent the night listening to picket reports, studying maps, and writing orders. General Braxton Bragg began attacking Yankees under General Jacob Cox's command.

General Hampton said, "We must destroy Cox before he links up with General Sherman, who is moving his army toward Goldsboro."

THURSDAY/9. Jesse asked Quartermaster, "How much forage do we have?"

"Are you kidding? Look at this very poor country. You know that General Wheeler's command is marching towards Fayetteville?"

"Yeah. Thanks." Jesse shouted, "Company C. Mount up."

Rain began pouring. Jesse galloped; then ran the horses for eight miles. At 9:00 P.M. they discovered the enemy's pickets and captured every one without firing a shot. A little farther and they captured a scouting party.

FRIDAY/10. Slowly and carefully the company moved to within one and a half miles of the Yankee camps and remained until daybreak. Rebels yelled and flowed into Yankee camps where most of the men were asleep.

Rebels captured six hundred prisoners. Another two hundred lay dead or wounded. Rebel losses were small. Jesse released 150 prisoners. "All right, Boys. We are not able to hold their camp on account of this muddy ground. Fall in. File formation. Move out."

They crossed a muddy creek and camped within six miles of Fayetteville. Jesse told some of the boys, "Y'all nearly captured General Judson Kilpatrick with his pants down."

SUNDAY/12. Only three miles from Fayetteville, North Carolina, Yanks attacked the Rebel Cavalry. They skirmished all day. Company C camped ten miles from said place. A rider told Jesse,

"Some of General Sherman's soldiers are busy in Fayetteville, destroying all transport facilities, machinery and industries that we might use."

TUESDAY/14. The Rebel cavalry regiment rode picket on the South River fifteen miles east of Fayetteville. Jesse said, "Yankee General Jacob Cox' troops are in Kingston, moving toward Goldsboro. Why do you suppose they're repairing railroad lines as they go?"

"Those lines provide a short supply route to the coast." Al pointed to a map.

WEDNESDAY/15. The Yanks attacked these pickets killing one man and wounding another. General Sherman moved his troops out of Fayetteville. Jesse said, "General Joe Johnston is trying to concentrate our Rebels north of General Sherman's advance."

Al said, "The Union Army is moving northward in three columns. Fighting broke out at Smith's Mill on Black River."

THURSDAY/16. Riding the Goldsboro Road twenty-five miles east of Fayetteville, Company C met and skirmished the Yanks. During that night Rebel General Hardee moved his troops to Bentonville to rejoin General Johnston's' main body.

FRIDAY/17. Jesse said, "This is a beautiful morning here in camps, thirty-three miles from Fayetteville."

"Yeah. It's poor country but a little better than usual." Al sat on the ground.

SATURDAY/18. Company C met up with General Wade Hampton. General Henry Slocum, leading Sherman's left wing, approached Bentonville. General Hampton's Rebels attacked the Yankees. Jesse said, "I think General Hampton is trying to slow down the Yanks' advance until General Johnston has time to concentrate forces at Bentonville."

"That makes sense to me." Al ate hard tack.

A DO OR DIE GAMBLE

Sunday/19. The Rebel Cavalry moved only three miles east, while the left wing of Sherman's Army, under General Slocum, marched toward Bentonville, they clashed, man-to-man, with General Hampton's riders. The Rebels fell back.

General Joe Johnston came up with his 18,000 men. An all out fight began at 10:00 A.M. and lasted all day. The Rebel counterattack forced the Yanks to fall back and entrench. Slocum's men repulsed several full-scale assaults before dark. During the night General Johnston's men fortified their positions opposite the Yanks.

MONDAY/20. The other two columns of Sherman's Army arrived and concentrated against Johnston's forces. Jesse skirmished all day. A Yank's minnie-ball killed E. A. Turner.

Jesse said, "I'm certain that General Johnston hoped to defeat General Slocum's troops before all these other Yankee troops arrived."

Al frowned. "And now our 20,000 men are facing an enemy army of nearly 100,000. It looks bad."

TUESDAY/21. The XVII Army Corps flanked the Rebel Cavalry and General Butler's Brigade stampeded. When General Johnston's forces came, a dreadful fight lasted all night.

Jesse said, "General Johnston is making a do-or-die gamble. He's concentrating his meager forces at Bentonville and attacking the Yankee's left wing savagely, hoping to drive away General Sherman."

Al drew a line in the sand. "Our pickets detected a Yankee force marching to Mill Creek Bridge, which could cut off our retreat. General Johnston has ordered our troops to withdraw to Smithfield."

"All right. General Sherman's two wings have united and are driving us from the field."

WEDNESDAY/22. Company C fell back and crossed the Neuse River near Smithfield. While setting up camp at said place, Jesse packed tobacco into a corncob pipe. "We just marched over the worst road I ever saw."

"Maybe you're just tired." Al smiled.

THURSDAY/23. Rebel Cavalry marched toward Goldsboro. Sherman's Army swarmed in the city where General Schofield's forces had already arrived from the coast. Company C met the enemy eight miles from said place and skirmished. The company camped on Atkin's Farm.

FRIDAY/24. They rode to the front to reconnoiter. They skirmished. Jesse killed three negroes. The company rode back to Atkin's Farm and camped.

SATURDAY/25. Jesse remained in camps all day. He washed clothes in a bucket of hot water. As he stepped into a pair of clean trousers he told Al, "This is the first day in eleven that I changed clothes and rested."

"I think we need to rest and organize our thoughts. We're going to face a big enemy soon and we'll stretch our minds and bodies to their limits."

"There are some letters long overdue." Jesse sharpened a stubby pencil with his knife.

SUNDAY/26. Company C remained in camps. Walking from a Chaplain's tent, Jesse said, "He preached a good sermon. Quite often, after I hear good sermons, I think about home, sweet home, and the loved ones there."

"Like Sallie Denton?" Al smiled.

"Aw. Sallie is just a little girl. She's been writing letters to me ever since I joined the Cavalry."

Quartermaster told Jesse, "General Lee assigned troops from General Richard Anderson and A. P. Hill's Corps, plus a division of W. H. F. Lee's Cavalry to General John Gordon. At 4:00 A.M., that force attacked Fort Stedman, just north of Petersburg. By 7:30 Lee ordered Gordon to withdraw. Rebels lost 4000 men killed and wounded, or captured."

"Oh, No. We can't continue loosing that many men." Jesse walked away.

MONDAY/27. Company C rode from Atkin's Farm. A large Rebel force relieved General Allen's Division on the Smithfield & Goldsboro Road.

TUESDAY/28. Jesse rode picket six miles from Goldsboro.

WEDNESDAY/29. Riders relieved Company C and they returned to camps.

THURSDAY/30. Jesse remained in camps. He patched a bridle. He punched a hole in a stirrup strap and pieced it together with a leather thong.

FRIDAY/31. Yanks ran in the Rebel pickets. Jesse told Al, "What a beautiful morning. My mind is wafted back to by gone days."

"Can we forget these days of war?" Al turned away.

"I doubt it." Again, Jesse rode picket six miles from Goldsboro.

APRIL, 1865

SATURDAY/1. At 3:00 A.M., the picket ride was quite pleasant. Soon after daylight the V South Carolina relieved Company C. At camps Quartermaster told Jesse, "On 29, March, General Grant sent General Sheridan's cavalry to Dinwiddie Court House with instructions to take Five Forks."

"That's interesting. General Lee sent a dispatch to General Pickett, telling him, 'Hold Five Forks at all hazards.' Generals Picket and Fitzhugh Lee attended a fish fry provided by General Thomas Rosser. Pickett rode through enemy fire and reached his command, which was in full retreat. Fitzhugh Lee was unable to rejoin his command entirely. Yankee infantry and cavalry crushed our Rebels and took 3000 prisoners. The Southside Railroad is less than three miles away. That will collapse the western end of General Lee's defenses."

TUESDAY/4. Company C passed through Raleigh and camped two miles from there. Jesse told Al, "If we can reach Danville, Virginia, we may be able to link-up with General Lee."

"That's a tremendous 'IF.' On 2, April, General Grant's entire forty-mile front surged forward. General Lee telegraphed President Davis that all preparations be made for leaving Richmond. And the Yankees killed General A. P. Hill at Hatcher's Run." Al hesitated.

"They killed General Hill?"

"Yep. By noon the Yankees captured the entire line to the west except Forts Gregg and Whitworth. General Grant's forces surrounded Petersburg completely, except a small area to the north across the Appomattox River. That was General Lee's only escape route and he took it.

General Longstreet moved re-enforcements as quickly as he could, on the Weldon and Petersburg Railroad. But the old war-torn tracks failed to move troops fast enough. The Army of Northern Virginia's life depended on General Longstreet's coming and manning the defenses or else the war would end on Petersburg's streets.

"General Lee needed time—he needed two hours. General Longstreet came up. He secured the right and during the night, General Lee's Army retreated westward. The Yankees lost 42,000 men. The Rebels 28,000."

WEDNESDAY/5. Company C camped six miles from Raleigh. Jesse said, "Richmond has gone up. The cloud is dark for all Rebels."

Quartermaster sipped coffee. "It may be darker than you think. General Lee planned to follow the Richmond & Danville Railroad. It's his one remaining line to supply his army. If he can reach Danville, and we, with

General Johnston's Army of Tennessee can get there, chances are we can withstand General Grant's punishing attacks."

"I'll add fuel to your fire." Jesse frowned. "General Lee's half-starved, footsore army marched hopefully to the railroad at Amelia Court House. Their eyes didn't focus on boxcars, loaded with food but empty tracks. Their supply train from Danville continued on to Richmond. Yankees captured it.

"General Lee sent forage parties into the country side. One-by-one they returned and reported that the families suffered as did the army. There was no food.

"Grant's huge army moved after General Lee, who thought his smaller force could outdistance the enemy. Today General Sheridan's Cavalry rode into the Rebel's path. General Lee veered northwestward toward Lynchburg."

FRIDAY/7. Company C camped near Smithfield.

SATURDAY/8. They camped near their old camps eight miles from Goldsboro.

SUNDAY/9. On Palm Sunday they moved across the Little River and returned. Quartermaster said, "While General Lee's Army marched, Generals Anderson and Ewell's disorganized commands plodded wearily, struggling to keep up. Once the sun appeared on 6, April, the Rebel Army had to cross Sayler's Creek. Wagons that moved between Generals Ewell and Gordon were attacked frequently by skirmishers. General Ewell ordered his and General Anderson's troops to halt to let the wagons move past them.

General Sheridan's cavalry spotted the unprotected wagons in a gap. The wagons never had a chance. Hundreds burned. Others surrendered.

"There was a terrible mess-up in orders. Almost a third of the Rebel Army, 8000, surrendered at Saylor's Creek."

MONDAY/10. General Sherman's Army advanced on the Rebels. Some skirmishing broke out.

TUESDAY/11. The Rebel Cavalry passed through Smithfield. They set fire to, and watched the bridge burn, which spanned the Neuse River. Rebels raced hard against Yankees.

WEDNESDAY/12. At 3:00 A.M., Company C camped eight miles from Smithfield. Rebel pickets found part of Sherman's Army in their front. Company C succeeded in getting out. An all-out fight commenced at 9:00 A.M. Company C fought hard until dark. They camped within five miles of Raleigh. Jesse said, "Our squad lost five men today. The Yanks killed three and wounded two. We've got to move on to Hillsborough."

Quartermaster sipped coffee from a tin cup. "Listen to this. Around noon, President Davis and most of what remained of our Confederate Government pulled into the train station at Greensboro. Petersburg and Richmond are no more for us.

"General Beauregard told President Davis that General Joe Johnston's Army of Tennessee was losing ground steadily to General Sherman's Army."

Jesse said, "My understanding is that Generals Johnston and Beauregard met with President Davis and his cabinet in Greensboro this morning. Reports from the North seem to make it certain that General Lee's Army is just about taken."

THURSDAY/13. Company C fell back through Raleigh. Since approximately 7:30 A.M., General Sherman, riding with his XIV Corps, entered Raleigh. Al frowned. "Only two of the eleven capitals of the seceding states remain in Confederate hands."

"We'll fight to the end." Jesse tied a piece of leather around the front of a stirrup.

FRIDAY/14. Company C mounted up and rode toward Hillsborough. Sherman's Army did not pursue. That night the company camped within seven miles of Hillsborough.

SATURDAY/15. Company C reached Hillsborough. Quartermaster looked to the ground. His words sounded muffled. "Almost everything General Lee's Army needed was on railcars—parked at Appomattox Court House. The Army of Northern Virginia never did get them.

"Soon after sunrise on 12, April, Union Troops lined up along the main road, running through Appomattox. 28,000 Confederate Soldiers, led by General John Gordon, marched along that road. They lay down their arms. I can just about hear the shifting of Yankee weapons when they held their rifles in the salute position.

"General Gordon accepted their salute and commanded his troops to return it."

Jesse's eyes moved from man to man. "You boys all have gloomy countenances and I guess I do, too. Our 30,000 Rebel Troops can hardly hope to defeat General Sherman's 80,000."

IT IS THE BENNITT'S FARM

Sunday/16. In camps Jesse told his boys, "This is the most unpleasant day I have spent in all my life. General Johnston obtained permission from President Davis to arrange a truce with General Sherman. The generals agreed to meet 17, April, at Durham Station. And it's true that President Lincoln was shot and killed while he attended a theater on the evening of 14, April."

The generals sat in these chairs

MONDAY/17. Generals Joe Johnston and Wade Hampton rode with a flag of truce and met Generals Sherman and Kilpatrick at Durham Station. Quartermaster said, "When the generals met today, General Johnston suggested a nice farm he'd ridden by as the negotiation place. It's the Bennitt's Farm. While the generals talked, the Bennitts stayed in their log kitchen near the house."

TUESDAY/18. Jesse told Company C, "Another flag of truce on armistice was agreed upon for an indefinite period. While the Generals met in the Bennitt's front room, our Secretary of War, John Breckinridge, entered and proposed terms. General Sherman rejected them and wrote his own.

"The generals signed a memorandum and I'll try to remember how it read. They mandated an armistice, general amnesty for our personnel, disband all Confederate Armies, and deposit arms at Southern State Capitols, soldiers sign oaths to stop fighting against the United States. Let me think. Oh, yes. Existing state governments are to be recognized as valid after proper officials swear allegiance to the United States. Federal Courts are to be re-established, and the Confederate people will be restored to full United States citizenship. That's about all I remember."

Jesse wrote a letter to his mother, "I will not attempt to picture the horrible conditions of our troops. I will leave this for a more able pen than the feeble one which I wielded so weakly."

TUESDAY/25. Quartermaster told Jesse, "The papers say the new President of the United States, Andrew Johnson, turned down General Sherman's peace agreement with General Johnston."

"So what happens now?" Jesse sat on the ground.

"General Grant went to General Sherman's headquarters in Raleigh on 24, April. They advised Sherman that he exceeded his authority. The Union generals notified General Johnston that the truce will end in forty-eight hours."

"We will resume fighting 26, April?" Jesse bit a blade of dry grass.

"You got it. However, General Sherman and Johnston agreed to meet again 26, April."

WEDNESDAY/26. In the early morn, Quartermaster peeked into Jesse's tent. "Congratulations. Because you are a fortunate one who has a fine horse, General Johnston wants you to ride with the flag of truce."

Jesse brushed his boots until they were free of mud. He unrolled an almost clean uniform.

General Johnston told his escorts, "We'll ride eight miles from Hillsborough on the Raleigh Road and meet General Sherman at a nice farm belonging to a Mr. James Bennitt."

They tied their horses to a white oak by the farmer's well and walked across the Hillsborough-Raleigh Road, toward the house. Several Yankee soldiers stood outside. Two carried hay over their shoulders and fed some horses. Some horses stood hitched to a rail fence which surrounded the house. The gate creaked as men passed in and out.

Jesse's eyes walked across a hardwood floor to andirons which held an unburned log in the large stone fireplace. A white teapot stood alone on a hand-hewn mantel. A tied-back curtain, left of the fireplace, allowed warm sunlight into the room. On a hardwood table two candles burned in silver candle sticks. Two cane bottomed chairs waited for the generals. And a clock, hanging on a log wall, tik-tocked lazily.

General Johnston introduced the Bennitts who excused themselves and walked towards the log kitchen.

The clock struck twelve, noon. General Grant said, "Gentlemen, let's get started."

Jesse and several escorts waited outside. A Union Lieutenant walked to his horse and untied the saddlebag. With a pistol in his hand he smiled at the Rebels. "I found this at Columbia, laying on a tavern table. One of our boys ran off and left it. From experience I know the Confederate Cavalry has excellent pistols. When the generals walk out of that door this time our war will be over in practical terms. I'll swap this pistol or the one I'm wearing for a Confederate pistol."

"What about the ammunition that goes with it?" Jesse held the pistol and examined its chamber.

"I'll give a supply to you."

Rebels and Yanks gathered into a circle, placed pistols on the ground, and garbled talk followed. Men laughed and shook hands. Jesse counted 116 pistols swapped. During three hours of gas even some horses were swapped.

General Johnston walked from the Bennitt House and mounted his horse. After riding quietly for a while he said, "I know you boys spent some anxious time. We prepared agreements for a general surrender. The terms are nearly the same General Grant proposed to General Lee. Rolls of all officers and enlisted men will be prepared. Our arms, artillery and public property will be stacked, parked and turned over to the Union Army. The side-arms, personal baggage, and horses of each man are not included. We'll issue paroled prisoners passes to each man, permitting them to go to their homes and remain there, not to be disturbed by the United States authority as long as they observe their parole. The rebellion is over for us."

This machine printed their paroles

The surrender party rode into the Hillsborough Camps. "General Johnston surrendered today."

Jesse listened to a soldier. "I calculate that in the course of four years' fighting, about 3000 men have passed in and out of my unit's ranks. It's a sad sight to look at the ol' First Tennessee Regiment. A mere squad of noble and brave men gathered around the tattered flag they followed in every battle through this awful war. The flag is so bullet-riddled and torn it's just a few red and blue shreds, drooping. We'll stack it with our guns forever."

Company C rode towards Greensboro at 9:00 P.M.

THURSDAY/27. At daylight they rode into company shops. General Wade Hampton ordered an assembly. Men stacked their weapons and turned in public property.

"Company C, mount up." They rode into Greensboro. Jesse said, "Everyone is so quiet that our horses' hoof beats sound as if they are the clatter of drums."

Later, Al said, "What did you learn from General Hampton's speech?"

"He told us about our deportment as soldiers during the past four years. Also, he recited to us the glories we gained on by-gone days.

"He said that General Lee had been compelled to yield to overwhelming numbers and resources. General Lee wanted to avoid useless sacrifice of the rest of us.

"And by the terms of these paroles we can go home and stay. I plan to help with the cotton crop."

SUNDAY/30 Jesse washed clothes and wrote a note to his mother, "Oh, if I were at home, sweet home."

MAY, 1865

MONDAY/1. Jesse called out, "Company C, fall in." Wearing a clean uniform, he walked five paces to his left; five paces back. "Boys, each of us is a paroled prisoner of the United States Government. For us, there is no Confederate Army. No longer are we allowed to march as the Jeff Davis Legion of Mississippi Cavalry. We are civilians. I'm leaving Greensboro right now, heading for the Sunny South. Anyone who wants to come along is welcome."

Jesse spurred his horse into a gallop. His eyes drifted to the Headquarters Flag Pole. A United States flag waved gently. Tears streamed down his cheeks, onto his saddle.

Late that afternoon, looking at a church, Jesse said, "I'm grateful to the Yanks for allowing us to keep our horses and filling our packs with rations. Greensboro is only twelve miles from here. We'll stop and camp; then ride on tomorrow. I'm looking at a bunch of tired young men, who are much older than they ought to be. Your clothes are tattered and torn. You haven't bathed for days, but you are on your way home."

A young paroled infantryman walked along the road. He turned in and asked, "May I enter your camp?"

"Yeah. We're on our way to Mississippi and stopped here for the night. I'll get you something to eat and a cup of coffee." Jesse poured.

"My name is Private Palmer and I joined the Army of Northern Virginia at Appomattox Court House." He smiled. "If I'd a knowed they was coming there to fight the end of the war, I'd awaited for them. I joined up when I was seventeen."

"Were you at Appomattox when General Lee surrendered?"

"Yes, Sir. We was camped near New Hope Church. I seen a flag of truce ride by, but didn't nobody know what it meant. General Grant and General Lee met in Appomattox Court House. You men of Mississippi has learned by now that Virginia is different. You can come into a Court House and never set foot in the Court House. In other words, Appomattox Court House is the county seat. Well anyhow, the generals met in Mister Wilmer McLean's house."

"You must have lived through lots of action, being as how you were in General Lee's Army." Jesse poured more coffee into Palmer's empty cup.

The private broke off a small twig from a sweet gum tree, chewed on one end, and sat on the ground. "Not really. I missed some of the war in '62, because I got terrible sick and spent most of the year in Chimborazo and Danville Hospitals. Then I went with General Pickett's Division at Gettysburg. In all the smoke and noise I got separated. When the smoke cleared, I seen four Yanks with their rifles aimed at me. My ma and pa didn't raise no foolish child; so I held up my hands and surrendered. I spent a year and a half in prison. They'd let us read some newspapers.

"General Grant took over the Army of the Potomac. He was different from all the others. He didn't know when to quit. He kept coming at us. The others lasted three, maybe four months, and they'd leave, but not General Grant. He planned to kill or capture, or wear down.

"General Lee lost too many men. He stopped them Yanks every time, but he ran out of men. Y'all know how we swapped prisoners, so many of theirs for so many of ours. They told us to go home. Go our own way. Well. I went back to the 18th Virginia Regiment. It was worn out. It warn't no army no more. Their faces struck me. Rations were scarce. Some men ran off. There warn't no open fights, but we was all in trenches now, fifty yards apart. The Yanks would yell at us. We'd yell back. It was bad, dirty. Men were sick and hungry. We was worried 'bout the right flank and the supply line. General Grant kept stretching his lines longer, longer, and longer. Grant had more men.

"Rebs had no choice. It was rumored we'd go to Amelia Court House, link up forces from Richmond; then head south to General Joe Johnston and you boys. We marched to Amelia. Those mostly needed rations didn't get there. I didn't have nothing to eat for three days. Some had gone four. There wasn't nothing around the whole area.

"Our spirits was down, worn out. Our nerves were frayed. We scattered out. There was problems at night. We was skitterish. The Yanks' cavalry blocked our road, south. Their infantry followed. Our men had gave all they could. They couldn't go no farther. On the road was broken down carriages, wagons, and empty food boxes. General Ewell had 7000 men behind us. Some of the men went crazy, skeddaled off into the woods.

"We got a handful of corn. Most of us would die for General Lee, but some slipped out to go home. I almost did, but then I thought about going this far. I might as well go all the way. With Yank cavalry cross the road, the Rebs stayed at New Hope Church.

"Next morning, Palm Sunday, General Gordon marched through Appomattox Court House, charged our cavalry, and scattered them. There was a thick fog that morning. When it lifted, General Lee saw the Yanks. He knowed the dance was over. He figured he didn't have no chance. He and Colonel Marshal rode to the McLean House and waited for General Grant.

"After about two hours, General Lee come out. The men who were there knowed it was over. They could see it in his face, it was over. Most of us cried and we warn't ashamed neither. It wuz hard to face. We had gave all we had. They told us we'd have to turn in our muskets and promise not to fight no more. We could go home. They printed paroles in the tavern and our officers signed them.

"On the 12th, we formed ranks for our last march together. There warn't no talking. The Yanks fell in along the old Richmond & Lynchburg Stage Road. When we got close to them, we could hear them shifting their muskets. They saluted us and we saluted back. You can't grapple with someone for four years and not have some respect.

"We got to know each other pretty well. We halted, faced the Yanks. Each man stepped forward, stacked his musket, and then the flag bearers laid down their flags. The Army of the Potomac had to be good to beat the Army of Northern Virginia. General Grant sent word to quit fighting and go home. I ain't sure where he is now."

Jesse lay down and placed his head on his saddle. "If only we could have gotten to y'all . . . . OH! OH."

TUESDAY/2. They camped twenty-three miles from Greensboro.
WEDNESDAY/3. They camped near the Yadkin River.
THURSDAY/4. They passed through Salisbury, North Caroline.
FRIDAY/5. They continued to ride.
SATURDAY/6. They camped near Doleis Court House.

SUNDAY/7. They rode twenty-five miles from Doleis Court House.

MONDAY/8. They crossed the Broad River.

TUESDAY/9. They rode.

WEDNESDAY/10. They rode.

THURSDAY/11. They rode.

FRIDAY/12. They passed through Abbeville Court House, South Carolina. Jesse said, "Friends, this is a beautiful town. I'm sure we can get a good dinner; then ride, ride, ride."

SATURDAY/13. They rested on the banks of the Savannah, Georgia, River.

SUNDAY/14. They ate a good dinner with some fair daughters. They camped near Mollensville, Georgia.

MONDAY/15. They passed through Woodstock and Centerville, Georgia. They camped near Woodville. Jesse walked into a general store and asked the proprietor, "Sir, we've got about thirty hungry horses. Can you tell us where we can buy some forage?'

"I tell you, young man, forage is scarce around here. There ain't nothing but grazing. I'm sorry."

"Thank you."

TUESDAY/16. They got along fine. Jesse said to Al, "I want to get home bad."

"It's been a long time." Al smiled. "But it won't be long now."

FRIDAY/19. They passed through Griffin, Georgia.

SATURDAY/20. They camped four miles from Greenville, Georgia.

SUNDAY/21. They passed through La Grange, Georgia, a beautiful place.

TUESDAY/23. They camped near Young Soil.

WEDNESDAY/24. They rode to a ferry on the Cousa River and the operator said, "The cables are broke down and we can't run today. You can ride to Wetumka and cross."

"That's a day's ride, isn't it?" Jesse frowned.

THURSDAY/25. They crossed the Cousa at Wetumka, Alabama.

FRIDAY/26. They passed through Prattsville.

SUNDAY/28. They passed near Marion, Alabama.

WEDNESDAY/31. Jesse rode into the lane, at home. He thought: I've been absent four years lacking sixteen days. Oh what a glorious day.

Sallie Denton bound from the creaking porch screen. Her strong arms tightened around Jesse's neck. I've waited so long for you to come home."

Their bodies swayed in unison for an eternal moment. Jesse retrieved a blood stained rag doll from his shirt pocket. "If it weren't for Madge, I wouldn't be here today."

Sallie reached into a pocket on her dress. "I made a new Madge for you. She will keep you safe."

A river of tears wiggled through Jesse's dusty face. "Let me look at you. You have grown into a lovely young lady. I can't imagine anyone who would write so many letters to an old Rebel Soldier, and send cookies, and tell about love. Sallie, when you get old enough, will you marry me?"

"OH, JESSE. You know I will. It won't be long now."

Jesse removed a piece of wire from Madge and bent it into a ring. He placed it on her third finger, left hand. "I'll always love you."

Ma and Pa Sparkman stepped from behind the front door. Ma said, through tears, "We saw that. The horrors of this war are over."